THE NATURE OF
COLORADO

An Introduction to Familiar Plants, Animals & Natural Attractions

By James Kavanagh

Illustrations by Raymond Leung
Introduction by James C. Rettie

WATERFORD PRESS

Publisher's Cataloging in Publication Data
Kavanagh, James Daniel, 1960 -
The Nature of Colorado. An Introduction to Familiar Plants, Animals & Natural Attractions. Includes biographical references and index.
1. Natural History – Colorado. 2. Animals – Identification – Colorado.
3. Plants – Identification – Colorado. 4. Tourism – Colorado.

Library of Congress Catalog Card Number: 2020932816
ISBN 978-1-62005-374-4

The introductory essay, "BUT A WATCH IN THE NIGHT" by JAMES C. RETTIE is from FOREVER THE LAND by RUSSELL AND KATE LORD. Copyright © 1950 by Harper & Brothers, copyright renewed © 1978 by Russell and Kate Lord. Reprinted with permission of HarperCollins Publishers.

The maps in this guide are adapted from maps copyright © by the United States Geological Survey and are reproduced with permission.

Waterford Press' toll-free order/information line is (800) 434-2555.
Download product information from our website: www.waterfordpress.com.
E-mail: info@waterfordpress.com

While every attempt has been made to ensure the accuracy of the information in this guide, it is important to note that experts often disagree with one another regarding the common name, size, appearance, habitat, distribution and taxonomy of species. For permissions, or to share comments, e-mail editor@waterfordpress.com.

CONTENTS

To my sister and best friend,

Dolly

The Nature of Colorado is intended to provide novice naturalists with a pocket reference to the state's familiar and distinctive species of plants and animals and the outstanding natural attractions found in Colorado.

The guide's primary purpose is to introduce the reader to common plants and animals and to highlight the diversity of species found in Colorado. Its secondary purpose is to show how all species in each ecosystem found here – from swamps to alpine forests – depend on each other, directly and indirectly, for survival.

Environmental education begins when people learn to appreciate the plants and animals in their immediate environment. When they start to care about local species – which often begins by learning their names – they take the first step toward learning about and understanding their place as an animal within their ecosystem.

The guide opens with a brief introduction to evolution. This is not intended in any way to dispute creationism, but is merely intended to illustrate the similarities and differences between major groups of plants and animals and show when each appeared in geologic time. To study the fossil record is fascinating in and of itself, but one of the most stunning things it reveals is a number of transitional species that are intermediary between different classes of organisms.

The brilliant introductory essay by James C. Rettie provides a simplified view of the evolution of life on earth, and the role that man – the animal – has played to date.

J.D.K.

BUT A WATCH IN THE NIGHT

BY JAMES C. RETTIE

James C. Rettie wrote the following essay while working for the National Forest Service in 1948. In a flash of brilliance, he converted the statistics from an existing government pamphlet on soil erosion into an analogy for the ages.

OUT BEYOND OUR SOLAR SYSTEM there is a planet called Copernicus. It came into existence some four or five billion years before the birth of our earth. In due course of time it became inhabited by a race of intelligent men.

About 750 million years ago the Copernicans had developed the motion picture machine to a point well in advance of the stage that we have reached. Most of the cameras that we now use in motion picture work are geared to take twenty-four pictures per second on a continuous strip of film. When such film is run through a projector, it throws a series of images on the screen and these change with a rapidity that gives the visual impression of normal movement. If a motion is too swift for the human eye to see it in detail, it can be captured and artificially slowed down by means of the slow-motion camera. This one is geared to take many more shots per second – ninety-six or even more than that. When the slow motion film is projected at the normal speed of twenty-four pictures per second, we can see just how the jumping horse goes over a hurdle.

What about motion that is too slow to be seen by the human eye? That problem has been solved by the use of the time-lapse camera. In this one, the shutter is geared to take only one shot per second, or one per minute, or even one per hour – depending upon the kind of movement that is being photographed. When the time-lapse film is projected at the normal speed of twenty-four pictures per second, it is possible to see a bean sprout growing up out of the ground. Time-lapse films are useful in the study of many types of motion too slow to be observed by the unaided, human eye.

The Copernicans, it seems, had time-lapse cameras some 757 million years ago and they also had superpowered telescopes that gave them a clear view of what was happening upon this earth. They decided to make a film record of the life history of earth and to make it on the scale of one picture per year. The photography has been in progress during the last 757 million years.

In the near future, a Copernican interstellar expedition will arrive upon our earth and bring with it a copy of the time-lapse film. Arrangements will be made for showing the entire film in one continuous run. This will begin at midnight of New Year's eve and continue day and night without a single stop until midnight on December 31. The rate of projection will be 24 pictures per second. Time on the screen will thus seem to move at the rate of twenty-four years per second; 1,440 years per minute; 86,400 years per hour; approximately two million years per day and sixty-two million years per month. The normal lifespan of individual man will occupy about three seconds. The full period of earth history that will be unfolded on the screen (some 757 million years) will extend from what the geologists call the Pre-Cambrian times up to the present. This will, by no means, cover the full time-span of the earth's geological history but it will embrace the period since the advent of living organisms.

During the months of January, February and March the picture will be desolate and dreary. The shape of the land masses and the oceans will bear little or no resemblance to those that we know. The violence of geological erosion will be much in evidence. Rains will pour down on the land and promptly go booming down to the seas. There will be no clear streams anywhere except where the rains fall upon hard rock. Everywhere on the steeper ground the stream channels will be filled with boulders hurled down by rushing waters. Raging torrents and dry stream beds will keep alternating in quick succession. High mountains will seem to melt like so much butter in the sun. The shifting of land into the seas, later to be thrust up as new mountains, will be going on at a grand scale.

Early in April there will be some indication of the presence of single-celled living organisms in some of the warmer and sheltered coastal waters. By the end of the month it will be noticed that some of these organisms have become multicellular. A few of them, including the Trilobites, will be encased in hard shells.

Toward the end of May, the first vertebrates will appear, but they will still be aquatic creatures. In June about 60 percent of the land area that we know as North America will be under water. One broad channel will occupy the space where the Rocky Mountains now stand. Great deposits of limestone will be forming under some of the shallower seas. Oil and gas deposits will be in process of formation – also under shallow seas. On land there will be no sign of vegetation. Erosion will be rampant, tearing loose particles and chunks of rock and grinding them into sand and silt to be spewed out by the streams into bays and estuaries.

About the middle of July the first land plants will appear and take up the tremendous job of soil building. Slowly, very slowly, the mat of vegetation will spread, always battling for its life against the power of erosion. Almost foot by foot, the plant life will advance, lacing down with its root structures whatever pulverized rock material it can find. Leaves and stems will be giving added protection against the loss of the soil foothold. The increasing vegetation will pave the way for the land animals that will live upon it.

Early in August the seas will be teeming with fish. This will be what geologists call the Devonian period. Some of the races of these fish will be breathing by means of lung tissue instead of through gill tissues. Before the month is over, some of the lung fish will go ashore and take on a crude lizard-like appearance. Here are the first amphibians.

In early September the insects will put in their appearance. Some will look like huge dragonflies and will have a wing span of 24 inches. Large portions of the land masses will now be covered with heavy vegetation that will include the primitive spore-propagating trees. Layer upon layer of this plant growth will build up, later to appear as coal deposits. About the middle of this month, there will be evidence of the first seed-bearing plants and the first reptiles. Heretofore, the land animals will have been amphibians that could reproduce their kind only by depositing a soft egg mass in quiet waters. The reptiles will be shown to be freed from the aquatic bond because they can reproduce by means of a shelled egg in which the embryo and its nurturing liquids are sealed and thus protected from destructive evaporation. Before September is over, the first dinosaurs will be seen – creatures destined to dominate the animal realm for about 140 million years and then to disappear.

In October there will be series of mountain uplifts along what is now the eastern coast of the United States. A creature with feathered limbs – half bird and half reptile in appearance – will take itself into the air. Some small and rather unpretentious animals will be seen to bring forth their young in a form that is a miniature replica of the parents and to feed these young on milk secreted by mammary glands in the female parent. The emergence of this mammalian form of animal life will be recognized as one of the great events in geologic time. October will also witness the high-water mark of the dinosaurs – creatures ranging in size from that of the modern goat to monsters like Brontosaurus that weighed some 40 tons. Most of them will be placid vegetarians, but a few will be hideous-looking carnivores, like Allosaurus and Tyrannosaurus. Some of the herbivorous dinosaurs will be clad in bony armor for protection against their flesh-eating comrades.

November will bring pictures of a sea extending from the Gulf of Mexico to the Arctic in space now occupied by the Rocky Mountains. A few of the reptiles will take to the air on bat-like wings. One of these, called Pteranodon, will have a wingspread of 15 feet. There will be a rapid development of the modern flowering plants, modern trees and modern insects. The dinosaurs will disappear. Toward the end of the month there will be a tremendous land disturbance in which the Rocky Mountains will rise out of the sea to assume a dominating place in the North American landscape.

As the picture runs on into December it will show the mammals in command of the animal life. Seed-bearing trees and grasses will have covered most of the land with a heavy mantle of vegetation. Only the areas newly thrust up from the sea will be barren. Most of the streams will be crystal clear. The turmoil of geological erosion will be confined to localized areas. About December 25 will begin the cutting of the Grand Canyon of the Colorado River. Grinding down through layer after layer of sedimentary strata, this stream will finally expose deposits laid down in Pre-Cambrian times. Thus in the walls of that canyon will appear geological formations dating from recent times to the period when the earth had no living organisms upon it.

The picture will run on through the latter days of December and even up to its final day with still no sign of mankind. The spectators will become alarmed in the fear that man has somehow been left out. But not so; sometime about noon on December 31 (one million years ago) will appear a stooped, massive creature of man-like proportions. This will be Pithecanthropus, the Java ape man. For tools and weapons he will have nothing but crude stone and wooden clubs. His children will live a precarious existence threatened on the one side by hostile animals and on the other by tremendous climatic changes. Ice sheets – in places 4,000 feet deep – will form in the northern parts of North America and Eurasia. Four times this glacial ice will push southward to cover half the continents. With each advance the plant and animal life will be swept under or pushed southward. With each recession of the ice, life will struggle to re-establish itself in the wake of the retreating glaciers. The woolly mammoth, the musk ox and the caribou all will fight to maintain themselves near the ice line. Sometimes they will be caught and put into cold storage – skin, flesh, blood, bones and all.

The picture will run on through supper time with still very little evidence of man's presence on earth. It will be about 11 o'clock when Neanderthal man appears. Another half hour will go by before the appearance of Cro-Magnon man living in caves and painting crude animal pictures on the walls of his dwelling. Fifteen minutes more will bring Neolithic man, knowing how to chip stone and thus produce sharp cutting edges for spears and tools. In a few minutes more it will appear that man has domesticated the dog, the sheep and, possibly, other animals. He will then begin the use of milk. He will also learn the arts of basket weaving and the making of pottery and dugout canoes.

The dawn of civilization will not come until about five or six minutes before the end of the picture. The story of the Egyptians, the Babylonians, the Greeks and the Romans will unroll during the fourth, the third and the second minute before the end. At 58 minutes and 43 seconds past 11:00 P.M. (just 1 minute and 17 seconds before the end) will come the beginning of the Christian era. Columbus will discover the new world 20 seconds before the end.

The Declaration of Independence will be signed just 7 seconds before the final curtain comes down.

In those few moments of geologic time will be the story of all that has happened since we became a nation. And what a story it will be! A human swarm will sweep across the face of the continent and take it away from the [Native Americans]. They will change it far more radically than it has ever been changed before in a comparable time. The great virgin forests will be seen going down before ax and fire. The soil, covered for eons by its protective mantle of trees and grasses, will be laid bare to the ravages of water and wind erosion. Streams that had been flowing clear will, once again, take up a load of silt and push it toward the seas. Humus and mineral salts, both vital elements of productive soil, will be seen to vanish at a terrifying rate.

The railroads and highways and cities that will spring up may divert attention, but they cannot cover up the blight of man's recent activities. In great sections of Asia, it will be seen that man must utilize cow dung and every scrap of available straw or grass for fuel to cook his food. The forests that once provided wood for this purpose will be gone without a trace. The use of these agricultural wastes for fuel, in place of returning them to the land, will be leading to increasing soil impoverishment. Here and there will be seen a dust storm darkening the landscape over an area a thousand miles across. Man-creatures will be shown counting their wealth in terms of bits of printed paper representing other bits of a scarce but comparatively useless yellow metal that is kept buried in strong vaults. Meanwhile, the soil, the only real wealth that can keep mankind alive on the face of this earth is savagely being cut loose from its ancient moorings and washed into the seven seas.

We have just arrived upon this earth. How long will we stay?

Because this guide has been written for the novice, every attempt has been made to simplify presentation of the material. Illustrations are accompanied by brief descriptions of key features, and technical terms have been held to a minimum. Plants and animals are arranged more-or-less in their taxonomic groupings. Exceptions have been made when nontraditional groupings facilitate field identification for the novice (e.g., wildflowers are grouped by color).

ILLUSTRATIONS

The majority of animal illustrations show the adult male in its breeding coloration. Plant illustrations are designed to highlight the characteristics that are most conspicuous in the field. It is important to note that illustrations are merely meant as guidelines; coloration, size and shape will vary depending on age, sex or season.

SPECIES CHECKLISTS

The species checklists at the back of this book are provided to allow you to keep track of the plants and animals you identify.

TIPS ON FIELD IDENTIFICATION

Identifying a species in the field can be as simple as one, two, three:

1. Note key markings, characteristics and/or behaviors;
2. Find an illustration that matches; and
3. Read the text to confirm your sighting.

Identifying mammals or birds in the field is not fundamentally different than identifying trees, flowers or other forms of life. It is simply a matter of knowing what to look for. Reading the introductory text to each section will make you aware of key characteristics of each group and allow you to use the guide more effectively in the field.

N.B. – We refer primarily to familiar species in this guide and do not list all species within any group. References listed in the bibliography at the back of this guide provide more detailed information about specific areas of study.

SPECIES DESCRIPTION

The species descriptions have been fragmented to simplify presentation of information:

① BROAD-TAILED HUMMINGBIRD

② *Selasphorus platycercus*

③ Size: 4–5 in. (10–13 cm)

④ Description: Small, iridescent green bird has a rose red throat and a broad tail. Note white line under its bill.

⑤ Habitat: Meadows, grasslands from the plains to the timberline.

⑥ Comments: Wings produce a cricket-like trilling sound in flight.

① COMMON NAME

The name in bold type indicates the common name of the species. It is important to note that a single species may have many common names.

② *Scientific Name*

The italicized Latin words refer to an organism's scientific name, a universally accepted two-part term that precisely defines its relationship to other organisms. The first capitalized word, the genus, refers to groups of closely related organisms. The second term, the species name, refers to organisms that look similar and interbreed freely. If the second word in the term is 'spp.', this indicates there are several species in the genus that look similar to the one illustrated. If a third word appears in the term, it identifies a subspecies, a group of individuals that are even more closely related.

③ Size

Generally indicates the maximum length of animals (nose to tail tip) and the maximum height of plants. Butterfly and moth measurements refer to wingspan. Exceptions are noted in the text.

④ Description

Refers to key markings and/or characteristics that help to distinguish a species.

⑤ Habitat

Where a species lives/can be found.

⑥ Comments

General information regarding distinctive behaviors, diet, vocalizations, related species, etc.

EVOLUTION OF ANIMALS

Animals are living organisms that can generally be distinguished from plants in four ways:

1. They feed on plants and other animals;
2. They have a nervous system;
3. They can move freely and are not rooted; and
4. Their cells do not have rigid walls or contain chlorophyll.

All animals are members of the animal kingdom, a group consisting of more than a million species. Species are classified within the animal kingdom according to their evolutionary relationships to one another.

Most of the animals discussed in this guide are members of the group called vertebrates. They all possess backbones and most have complex brains and highly developed senses.

The earliest vertebrates appeared in the oceans about 500 million years ago. Today, surviving species are divided into five main groups:

1. Fishes
2. Amphibians
3. Reptiles
4. Birds
5. Mammals

Following is a simplified description of the evolution of the vertebrates and the differences between groups.

FISHES

The oldest form of vertebrate life, fishes evolved from invertebrate sea creatures 400–500 million years ago. All are cold-blooded (ectothermic) and their activity levels are largely influenced by the surrounding environment.

The first species were armored and jawless and fed by filtering tiny organisms from water and mud. Surviving members of this group include lampreys and hagfishes. Jawless fishes were succeeded by jawed fishes that quickly came to dominate the seas, and still do today. The major surviving groups include:

1. **Sharks and rays** – more primitive species that possess soft skeletons made of cartilage; and
2. **Bony fishes** – a more advanced group of fishes that have bony skeletons, it includes most of the fishes currently existing.

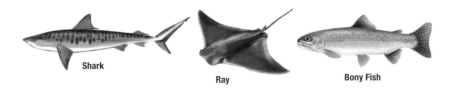

Shark

Ray

Bony Fish

Physiological Characteristics of Fishes

- **Heart and gills**
  A two-chambered heart circulates the blood through a simple system of arteries and veins. Gills act like lungs and allow fishes to absorb dissolved oxygen from the water into their bloodstream.

- **Nervous system**
  Small anterior brain is connected to a spinal cord that runs the length of the body.

- **Digestive system**
  Digestive system is complete. A number of specialized organs produce enzymes that help to break down food in the stomach and intestines. Kidneys extract urine from the blood and waste is eliminated through the anus.

- **Reproduction**
  In most fishes, the female lays numerous eggs in water and the male fertilizes them externally. Young usually hatch as larvae, and the larval period ranges from a few hours to several years. Survival rate of young is low.

- **Senses**
  Most have the senses of taste, touch, smell, hearing and sight, although their vision is generally poor. Fishes hear and feel by sensing vibrations and temperature and pressure changes in the surrounding water.

AMPHIBIANS

The first limbed land-dwellers, amphibians evolved from fishes 300–400 million years ago and became the dominant land vertebrates for more than 100 million years. Like fishes, amphibians are cold-blooded and their activity levels are largely influenced by the environment.

The first fish-like amphibian ancestors to escape the water were those that had the ability to breathe air and that possessed strong, paired fins that allowed them to wriggle onto mud-flats and sandbars. (Living relics of this group include five species of lungfish and the rare coelacanth.) Although amphibians were able to exploit rich new habitats on land, they remained largely dependent on aquatic environments for survival and reproduction.

The major surviving groups are:

1. **Salamanders** – slender-bodied, short-legged, long-tailed creatures that live secretive lives in dark, damp areas; and
2. **Frogs and toads** – squat-bodied animals with long hind legs, large heads and large eyes. Frogs are smooth skinned, toads have warty skin.

Salamander

Frog

Toad

Advances made over fishes

- **Lungs and legs**
  By developing lungs and legs, amphibians were freed from the competition for food in aquatic environments and were able to flourish on land.

- **Improved circulatory system**
  Amphibians' heart evolved with three chambers that enhanced gas exchange in the lungs and provided body tissues with highly oxygenated blood.

- **Ears**
  Frogs and toads developed external ears that enhanced their hearing ability, an essential adaptation to survive on land.

- **Reproduction**
  Most amphibians reproduce like fish. Salamanders differ in that most fertilize eggs internally rather than externally. In many, the male produces a sperm packet that the female collects and uses to fertilize eggs as they are laid.

REPTILES

Reptiles appeared 300–350 million years ago. They soon dominated the earth and continued to rule the land, sea and air for more than 130 million years. Cold-blooded like amphibians, reptiles evolved a host of characteristics that made them better suited for life on land.

About 65 million years ago, the dominant reptiles mysteriously underwent a mass extinction. A popular theory suggests this was caused by a giant meteor hitting the earth that sent up a huge dust cloud that blotted out the sun. The lack of sun and subsequently low temperatures caused many plants and animals to perish.

The major surviving reptilian groups are:

1. **Turtles** – hard-shelled reptiles with short legs;
2. **Lizards** – scaly-skinned reptiles with long legs and tails;
3. **Snakes** – long, legless reptiles with scaly skin; and
4. **Crocodilians** – very large reptiles with elongate snouts, toothy jaws and long tails.

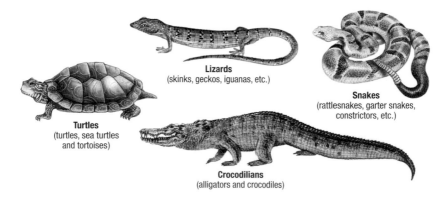

Lizards
(skinks, geckos, iguanas, etc.)

Snakes
(rattlesnakes, garter snakes, constrictors, etc.)

Turtles
(turtles, sea turtles and tortoises)

Crocodilians
(alligators and crocodiles)

Advances Made Over Amphibians

- **Dry, scaly skin**
  Their dry skin prevents water loss and also protects them from predators.

- **Posture**
  Many reptiles evolved an upright posture and strong legs that enhanced their mobility on land.

- **Improved heart and lungs**
  Their heart and lungs were more efficient, which heightened their activity levels. The heart had four chambers – although the division between ventricles was usually incomplete – making it less likely that oxygenated and deoxygenated blood would mix.

- **Defense**
  They were agile and better able to defend themselves, having sharp claws and teeth or beaks capable of inflicting wounds.

BIRDS

Birds evolved from reptiles 100–200 million years ago. Unlike species before them, birds were warm-blooded (endothermic) and able to regulate their body temperature internally.* This meant that they could maintain high activity levels despite fluctuations in environmental temperature. They are believed to have evolved from a group of gliding reptiles, with their scaly legs considered proof of their reptilian heritage.

Birds come in a vast array of groups. All have feathered bodies, beaks, lack teeth and have forelimbs modified into wings. Most can fly.

Advances Made Over Reptiles

- **Ability to fly**
  By evolving flight, birds were able to exploit environments that were inaccessible to their competitors and predators. The characteristics they evolved that allowed them to fly included wings, feathers, hollow bones and an enhanced breathing capacity.

- **Warm-blooded**
  An insulating layer of feathers enhanced their capacity to retain heat. They also had true four-chambered hearts that enhanced their ability to maintain high activity levels in varying environments.

- **Keen senses**
  Birds evolved very keen senses of vision and hearing and developed complex behavioral and communicative patterns.

- **Reproduction**
  Fertilization was internal and the eggs had hard, rather than leathery, shells. Unlike most reptiles, birds incubated their eggs themselves and protected and nurtured their young for a period of time following birth.

* There is still a debate over whether or not some dinosaurs were warm-blooded.

MAMMALS

Mammals evolved from reptiles 100–200 million years ago. Though warm-blooded like birds, they are believed to have different reptilian ancestors. In addition to being warm-blooded, mammals also evolved physiological adaptations that allowed them to hunt prey and avoid predation better than their competitors.

Mammals rapidly exploited the habitats left vacant by the dinosaurs and have been the dominant land vertebrates for the past 65 million years. Man is a relatively new addition to the group, having a lineage of less than 3 million years.

Mammals have evolved into three distinct groups, all of which have living representatives:

1. **Monotremes** – egg-laying mammals;
2. **Marsupials** – pouched mammals that bear living, embryonic young; and
3. **Placentals** – mammals that bear fully-developed young.

Monotremes
(platypus and echidna)

Marsupials
(opossums, kangaroos etc.)

Placentals
(squirrels, humans,
dogs, rats etc.)

Advances Made Over Birds

- **Reproduction**
  Fertilization was internal, but in most, the young developed in the female's uterus instead of an egg. After birth, the young were fed and nurtured by adults for an extensive period, during which they learned behavioral lessons from their elders and siblings. This emphasis on learned responses at an early age is believed to have contributed to the superior intelligence and reproductive success of the group.

- **Hearing**
  Most had three bones in the middle ear to enhance hearing. (Birds and reptiles have one.)

- **Teeth**
  Many developed specialized teeth that allowed them to rely on a variety of food sources. Incisors were for cutting, canines for tearing and molars for chewing or shearing.

- **Breathing**
  Mammals evolved a diaphragm that increased breathing efficiency.

- **Posture**
  Many evolved long, strong legs and were very agile on land.

EVOLUTION OF PLANTS

Plants are living organisms that can generally be distinguished from animals in four ways:

1. They synthesize their own food from carbon dioxide, water and sunlight;
2. They do not have a nervous system;
3. Most are rooted and cannot move around easily; and
4. Their cells have rigid walls and contain chlorophyll, a pigment needed for photosynthesis.

All plants are members of the plant kingdom. According to the fossil record, plants evolved from algae that originated nearly 3 billion years ago. Since then, plants have evolved into millions of species in a mind-boggling assortment of groups.

Most North American plants are classified into two main groups:

1. **Gymnosperms** – plants with naked seeds; and
2. **Angiosperms** – flowering plants with enclosed seeds

Gymnosperms   Angiosperms

GYMNOSPERMS – THE NAKED SEED PLANTS

This group of mostly evergreen trees and shrubs includes some of the largest and oldest known plants. They began to appear around 300–400 million years ago and were the dominant plant species on earth for nearly 200 million years. The most successful surviving group of gymnosperms are the conifers, which include such species as pines, spruces, firs, larches and junipers.

Most conifers are evergreen and have small needle-like or scale-like leaves that are adapted to withstand extreme temperature changes. Some species are deciduous (leaf shedders), but most retain their leaves for two or more years before shedding them.

Reproduction

Most conifers produce cones – wood-like fruits that contain the male and female gametes. The male cones produce pollen that is carried by the wind to settle between the scales of female cones on other trees. The pollen stimulates ovules to change into seeds, and the scales of the female cone close up to protect the seeds. When the seeds are ripe, up to two years later, environmental conditions stimulate the cone to open its scales and the naked seeds to fall to the ground.

ANGIOSPERMS – THE FLOWERING PLANTS

Angiosperms first appeared in the fossil record around 130 million years ago. They quickly adapted to a wide variety of environments and succeeded gymnosperms as the dominant land plants. Their reproductive success was largely due to two key adaptations:

Advances made over gymnosperms

1. They produced flowers that attracted pollinating agents such as insects and birds; and
2. They produced seeds encased in fruits to aid in seed dispersal.

Angiosperms are classified in two main groups:

1. **Monocots** – plants with one embryonic leaf at germination, parallel-veined leaves, stems with scattered vascular bundles with little or no cambium (group includes grasses, cattails, orchids and corn); and
2. **Dicots** – plants with two embryonic leaves at germination, net-veined leaves, stems with cylindrical vascular bundles in a regular pattern that contain cambium (group includes more than 200,000 species ranging from tiny herbs to huge trees).

Angiosperms make up a diverse and widespread group of plants ranging from trees and shrubs such as oaks, cherries, maples, hazelnuts and apples, to typical flowers like lilies, orchids, roses, daisies and violets. The trees and shrubs within this group are commonly referred to as deciduous and most shed their leaves annually.

Reproduction

A typical flower has colorful petals that encircle the male and female reproductive structures (see illustration p. 123). The male stamens are composed of thin filaments that support anthers containing pollen. The female pistil contains unfertilized seeds in the swollen basal part called the ovary. Pollination occurs when pollen, carried by the wind or animals, reaches the pistil.

Once fertilization has occurred, the ovules develop into seeds and the ovary into a fruit. The fruit and seeds mature together, with the fruit ripening to the point where the seeds are capable of germinating. At maturity, each seed contains an embryo and a food supply to nourish it upon germination. Upon ripening, the fruit may fall to the ground with the seeds still inside, as in peaches, cherries and squash, or it may burst open and scatter its seeds in the wind, like poplar trees, willows and dandelions.

Fruit comes in many forms, from grapes, tomatoes, apples and pears, to pea and bean pods, nuts, burrs and capsules. Regardless of its shape, fruit enhances the reproductive success of angiosperms in two important ways. First, it helps to protect the seeds from the elements until they have fully matured, enabling them to survive unfavorable conditions. Second, fruit aids in seed dispersal. Some fruits are eaten by animals that eventually release the seeds in their feces, an ideal growing medium. Others may be spiny or burred so they catch on the coats of animals, or may have special features that enable them to be carried away from their parent plant by the wind or water.

GEOLOGICAL TIMESCALE

ERA	PERIOD	MYA*	EVENTS
CENOZOIC	HOLOCENE	.01	Dominance of humans.
CENOZOIC	QUATERNARY	2.5	First human civilizations.
CENOZOIC	TERTIARY	65	Mammals, birds, insects and angiosperms dominate the land.
MESOZOIC	CRETACEOUS	135	Dinosaurs extinct. Mammals, insects and angiosperms undergo great expansion. Gymnosperms decline.
MESOZOIC	JURASSIC	190	Age of Reptiles; dinosaurs dominant. First birds appear.
MESOZOIC	TRIASSIC	225	First dinosaurs and mammals appear. Gymnosperms are dominant plants.
PALEOZOIC	PERMIAN	280	Great expansion of reptiles causes amphibians to decline. Many marine invertebrates become extinct.
PALEOZOIC	CARBONIFEROUS	340	Age of Amphibians; amphibians dominant. First reptiles appear. Fish undergo a great expansion.
PALEOZOIC	DEVONIAN	400	Age of Fishes; fishes dominant. First amphibians, insects and gymnosperms appear.
PALEOZOIC	SILURIAN	430	First jawed fishes appear. Plants move onto land.
PALEOZOIC	ORDOVICIAN	500	First vertebrates appear.
PALEOZOIC	CAMBRIAN	600	Marine invertebrates and algae abundant.

*Millions of years ago

GENERALIZED RELIEF

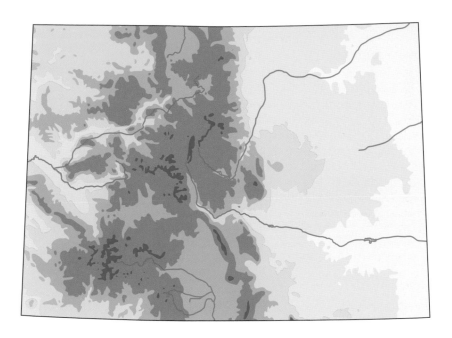

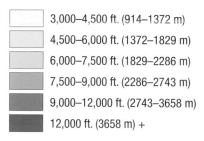

- 3,000–4,500 ft. (914–1372 m)
- 4,500–6,000 ft. (1372–1829 m)
- 6,000–7,500 ft. (1829–2286 m)
- 7,500–9,000 ft. (2286–2743 m)
- 9,000–12,000 ft. (2743–3658 m)
- 12,000 ft. (3658 m) +

GEOGRAPHY

Highest Point: 14,443 ft. (4,376 m) Mount Elbert

Area: 104,100 sq. mi. (156,150 sq. km)

Mountain Ranges

To many, Colorado is synonymous with the awe-inspiring Rocky Mountains, the great assemblage of mountain chains that traverse North America from Alaska to Mexico. The Colorado Rockies make up approximately 40% of the state's land area and include 5 major mountain ranges: The Front Range punctuated by 14,110 ft. (4300 m). Pikes Peak, the Park Range just beyond, the soaring Sawatch Range dominated by Mt. Elbert, the highest peak in all the Rockies and the imposing Sangre de Cristo Mountains and San Juan Mountains further south. Collectively these ranges are home to 54 mountains that rise 14,000 feet (4267 m) or higher, the most of any other state in the country. Another 830 peaks reach 11,000–14,000 ft. (3350–4267 m). The crest of this high terrain forms Colorado's portion of North America's Continental Divide.

Rivers

Six major rivers flow out of the Colorado Rockies, their upper reaches providing access to pristine wilderness, spectacular scenery and whitewater excitement. Rising on the western side of the Continental Divide is the mighty Colorado River. Joined by major tributaries such as the Gunnison, the Colorado is internationally famous for the deep, awesomely beautiful canyons it has carved in its (1,450 miles/2334 km) journey toward the Pacific Ocean. East of the Divide rise the headwaters of the Rio Grande, Arkansas, North and South Platte and Republican rivers. As with the Colorado, numerous dams on these waterways help meet the demands of burgeoning human populations.

Prairies

Colorado's landscape averages 6,800 feet (2073 m) above sea level, the highest mean elevation of any state. Even so, a broad swath of the Great Plains stretches east of the Colorado Rockies covering 40% of the state. Much of this flat, arid shortgrass prairie remains untouched, providing ample opportunities to explore the native plants and wildlife in a habitat that has disappeared elsewhere in the American West.

ECOSYSTEMS

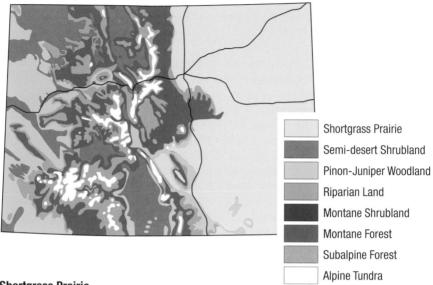

Shortgrass Prairie
Semi-desert Shrubland
Pinon-Juniper Woodland
Riparian Land
Montane Shrubland
Montane Forest
Subalpine Forest
Alpine Tundra

Shortgrass Prairie

Deep-rooted prairie grasses such as blue grama grass, buffalo grass and Indian grass are the dominant plants in this arid ecosystem, where annual rainfall only averages around 14 inches (35 cm) and many years are drier. Punctuating the broad expanses of grasslands are hardy shrubs including sagebrush and prickly pear cactus, as well as some drought-tolerant wildflowers. This dry ecosystem usually occurs below 5,500 ft. (1,670 m), although lush pockets exist at higher elevations in mountain valleys.

Semi-desert Shrubland

This almost desert-like ecosystem presents a rugged, often rocky landscape that typically receives no more than 10 in. (25 cm) of precipitation a year. Colorado's semi-desert shrublands occur at lower elevations on both sides of the Rockies, as well in several of the inter-mountain basins known locally as "parks". Too dry to support significant trees, this ecosystem may be dotted with big sagebrush or the similar saltbush and greasewood, cholla cactus and other drought tolerant plants.

Pinyon-Juniper Woodland

Trees resistant both to cold and moderate rainfall dominate this mid-elevation woodland ecosystem. The dominant vegetation in a pinyon-juniper woodland consists of pinyon pines or junipers that typically grow no taller than about 12 ft. (3.6 m), with individual trees separated by stretches of bare ground.

Riparian Land

Interspersed among other ecosystems are distinct natural communities in riparian environments – the often lush growth of trees, shrubs and other plant life along the edges of streams, rivers, lakes, ponds and wet meadows. At high elevations willows are the dominant large riparian-zone plants, while at mid-altitudes willows are interspersed with river birches, narrowleaf cottonwood, alders and blue spruces. Below about 6,000 ft. (1800 m) cottonwoods may tower over an understory of red-osier dogwoods and other species.

Montane Shrubland

In much of western and southern Colorado, low elevation grasslands and higher-altitude forests bracket thousands of acres of montane shrublands. These consist of dense thickets of mountain mahogany, Gambel oak, serviceberry, chokecherry and skunkbrush, among others. Dense, essentially pure stands of Gambel oaks cover some areas while elsewhere sagebrush joins the mix and seasonal wildflowers bloom profusely.

Montane Forest

Several types of low to mid-altitude montane forests cover vast stretches of Colorado where the elevation ranges from 6,000 to 9,000 ft. (1800–2700 m) and the average annual precipitation of 20–25 inches (50-63 cm) supports the growth of large trees. Ponderosa pine dominates up to about 8,000 feet (2400 m). At higher elevations the forest shifts to a mix of conifers including limber pine, bristlecone pine, blue spruce and Douglas-fir, often with an understory of mountain blueberry and other shrubs. Stands of lodgepole pine grade into the sub-alpine ecosystem that begins at around 9,000 ft. (2700 m). Huge stands of quaking aspens may cover hillsides.

Subalpine Forest [Spruce-fir Forest, Boreal Forest]

Engelmann spruce and Rocky Mountain fir dominate this ecosystem located above 9,000 ft. (2700 m). At or just above the nominal tree line of 11,400 ft. (3474 m), a zone sometimes called the krummholz, dwarfed, wind-contorted trees may be only a few feet tall after decades of growth. Often such trees have branches only on one side because ice and wind have ripped away buds on the opposite side.

Alpine Tundra

Alpine tundra occurs on both the eastern and western slopes of the Colorado Rockies, on rocky ridges and on mountaintops above the tree line at approximately 11,400 ft. (3474 m). It consists of bare rocks and rubble interspersed with plant species that form cushions or mats that can withstand the strong winds that routinely buffet this cold environment. Clumps of alpine avens may dot entire ridges and slopes along with low-growing herbs such as moss campion, mountain dandelion, mountain heaths and alpine varieties of sandwort, spring beauty and grasses. Bighorn sheep, pikas, weasels and martins may frequent the tundra through much of the year.

PRECIPITATION

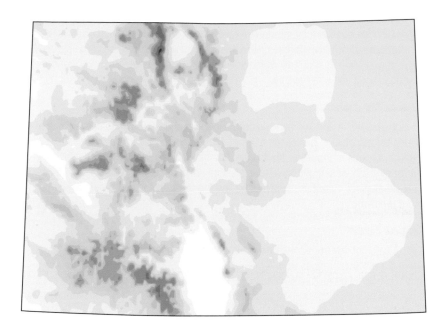

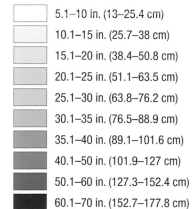

	5.1–10 in. (13–25.4 cm)
	10.1–15 in. (25.7–38 cm)
	15.1–20 in. (38.4–50.8 cm)
	20.1–25 in. (51.1–63.5 cm)
	25.1–30 in. (63.8–76.2 cm)
	30.1–35 in. (76.5–88.9 cm)
	35.1–40 in. (89.1–101.6 cm)
	40.1–50 in. (101.9–127 cm)
	50.1–60 in. (127.3–152.4 cm)
	60.1–70 in. (152.7–177.8 cm)

CLIMATE

Colorado's location well inland at mid-latitudes of North America endows the state generally with a Highland Continental climate marked by cold winters, hot summers, low humidity and low rainfall. Within this broad picture great climatic variations and extremes exist due to the state's overall high elevation and the influence of the Rocky Mountains. The Colorado Climate Center recognizes three basic climate regions: Eastern Plains, Mountains and Western Colorado. The following table gives a general overview of the weather patterns in each region.

Climate Region	Annual Precipitation			Annual Temperature		
	Max	Min	Avg	Max	Min	Avg
Eastern Plains	18 in.	10 in.	14 in.	115°F (46°C)	−15°F (−26°C)	50°F (10°C)
Mountains	60+ in.	7 in.	27 in.	88°F (31°C)	7°F (−13°C)	40°F (4°C)
Western Colorado	14 in.	8 in.	11 in.	95°F (35°C)	−50°F (−45°C)	60°F (15°C)

Sharp differences in elevation and mountain topography in Colorado mean that precipitation and temperatures may differ sharply over short distances. Recorded average annual precipitation, including snowfall, ranges from a high of 537 inches (136 m) in the southern Rockies to a low of 7 inches (18 cm) in the extreme southwest corner of the state. Mean annual temperatures for the state vary from 84° to 133° F (29° to 56° C). The temperature extremes vary from a high of 118° F (48° C) to a low of −61° F (−52° C).

Climate also varies greatly on the eastern and western slopes of the Colorado Rockies. Air masses arriving from the Pacific drop most of their moisture when they first encounter the high mountains, so much more rain and snow falls on west-facing slopes than on the eastern slopes. This rain shadow east of the Continental Divide extends throughout the eastern plains of Colorado and is a major factor in that region's semi-arid climate.

Dramatic extremes of temperature and precipitation profoundly affect the distribution and seasonal activity of Colorado's plants and animals. In the eastern prairie and arid western high desert, plants and animals have evolved physiological and behavioral traits that help them survive intense heat and periodic drought. At higher elevations where the growing season is short and temperatures regularly dip into the teens, annual plants flower and produce seeds quickly and perennials have adaptations that allow their tissues to withstand freezing. Among animals common survival adaptations include thick fur for insulation, hibernation and seasonal migrations.

Most mammals are warm-blooded, furred creatures that have 4 limbs and a tail, 5 digits on each foot and several different kinds of teeth. All North American species give birth to live young that feed on milk from their mother's mammary glands.

How to Identify Mammals

Mammals are generally secretive in their habits and therefore difficult to spot in the field. The best time to look for mammals is at dusk, dawn and at night, since many retreat to shelter during the day to escape the heat. Some of the best places to look for them are in undisturbed areas affording some source of cover such as wood edges and scrub thickets.

When you spot a mammal, consider its size, shape and color. Check for distinguishing field marks and note the surrounding habitat.

Common Tracks

Studying tracks is an easy way to discover the kinds of mammals found in your area. For more information on animal tracks, see bibliography references under mammals.

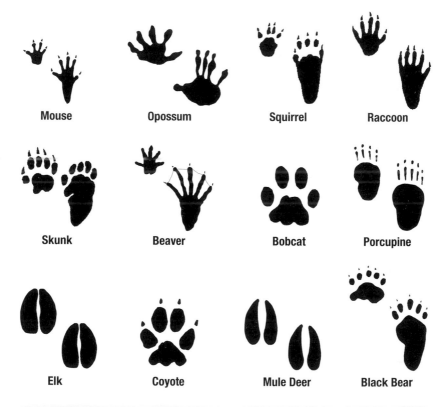

| Mouse | Opossum | Squirrel | Raccoon |

| Skunk | Beaver | Bobcat | Porcupine |

| Elk | Coyote | Mule Deer | Black Bear |

N.B. – Tracks are not to scale

MARSUPIALS

Related to kangaroos and koalas, the opossum is the only marsupial found in North America. Young are born prematurely and move to a fur-lined pouch (marsupium) where they complete their development attached to a teat.

VIRGINIA OPOSSUM
Didelphis virginiana

Size: 25–40 in. (63–100 cm)

Description: Grayish fur, white face, black-tipped ears and naked, rat-like tail.

Habitat: Woodlands, farming areas, forest edges, suburban areas.

Comments: Most active in the evening and at night. It has the peculiar habit of pretending to be dead ("playing possum") when frightened. One of the most common nuisance mammals in Colorado's urban areas.

SHREWS

These small mammals have long snouts, short legs, small eyes and ears and sharp teeth and 5 digits on the front and hind feet. They live on or under the ground and feed on insects and other invertebrates.

MASKED SHREW
Sorex cinereus

Size: To 4 in. (10 cm)

Description: Gray-brown, mouse-like mammal with a long, pointed nose and a long tail.

Habitat: Moist fields, bogs and woods.

Water Shrew

Comments: Active throughout the year, it is one of nine species of shrew found in Colorado. Like all shrews, it has a very high metabolic rate and must eat voraciously to stay alive. Another widespread Colorado shrew is the semi-aquatic water shrew (*S. palustris*). It has water-resistant fur and is often seen diving for prey along the shorelines of streams and lakes.

BATS

The only true flying mammals, bats have large ears, small eyes and broad wings. Primarily nocturnal, they have developed a sophisticated sonar system – echolocation – to help them hunt insects at night. As they fly, they emit a series of high frequency sounds that bounce off objects to tell them what lies in their path. During daylight, they seek refuge in caves, trees and attics. Rarely harmful, bats are important as pollinators and are valuable in helping check insect populations.

LITTLE BROWN BAT
Myotis lucifugus

Size: To 4 in. (10 cm)

Description: Small chocolate-brown bat with glossy fur.

Habitat: Variable throughout most of the state.

Comments: One of Colorado's most common and widespread bats, it is one of 17 species found here. Roosts in caves and buildings in small colonies during warmer months; the majority migrate south during winter. Other widespread Colorado bats include the similar, larger, big brown bat (*Eptesicus fuscus*) and the silver-tipped hoary bat (*Lasiurus cinereus*).

Big Brown Bat   Hoary Bat

BRAZILIAN FREE-TAILED BAT
Tadarida brasiliensis

Size: 4–5 in. (10–13 cm)

Description: Small chocolate-brown bat with velvety fur and a tail extending beyond the wing membrane.

Habitat: Roosts in caves and buildings.

Comments: More than 100,000 roost in an abandoned mine in the San Luis Valley and pour out like thick clouds each evening to feed.

TOWNSEND'S BIG-EARED BAT
Corynorhinus townsendii

Size: 3–5 in. (8–13 cm)

Description: Gray to brown bat has enormous ears.

Habitat: Pine-juniper forests and deserts.

Comments: Feeds primarily on moths. Hibernates in caves in winter.

RABBITS & ALLIES

Members of this distinctive group of mammals have long ears, large eyes and long hind legs. They commonly rest in protected areas like thickets during the day. When threatened, they thump their hind feet on the ground as an alarm signal.

DESERT COTTONTAIL
Sylvilagus audubonii

Size: 14–17 in. (35–43 cm)

Description: Coat is grayish above, white below. Note rusty nape and white tail. Large ears are black-tipped.

Habitat: Well-vegetated foothills, plains and canyons statewide up to 7,000 ft. (2100 m).

Comments: Active day and night, it feeds on a range of plants including grasses, mesquite and cacti. Often uses stumps and sloping trees as lookouts. The most abundant and commonly observed Colorado rabbit.

MOUNTAIN COTTONTAIL
Sylvilagus nuttallii

Size: 13–15 in. (33–38 cm)

Description: Small round bunny has short legs and dark ears. Fur is gray-brown above and light below.

Habitat: Coniferous forests, sagebrush flats.

Comments: Feeds primarily on grasses and shrubs at dawn and dusk. Active year-round.

SNOWSHOE HARE
Lepus americanus

Size: 16–20 in. (40-50 cm)

Description: Coat is brown to yellowish in summer and white in winter. Ears are black-tipped throughout the year. Large hind feet are well-furred to allow it to travel over deep snow.

Habitat: Primarily subalpine forests from 8,000–11,000 ft. (2400–3300 m).

Comments: Tracks of back feet in fresh snow can be up to 6 in. (15 cm) long and 10 ft. (3 m) apart. Also called the varying hare, it is most active at dusk and dawn. Feeds on grasses, buds, twigs and bark. A favorite prey for bobcats, snowshoe hare population fluctuations significantly affect the abundance of bobcats.

Summer

White

WHITE-TAILED JACKRABBIT
Lepus townsendii
Size: 20–25 in. (50–63 cm)

Description: Large gray or tan rabbit has black-tipped ears and a white tail. Coat is all-white in winter in northern Colorado.

Habitat: Open areas in deserts and grasslands.

Comments: Very athletic, it leaps up to 10 ft. (3 m) at a time and reaches burst speeds up to 35 mph (56 kph). Active in late afternoon and evening. The similar black-tailed jackrabbit (*L. californicus*) is also common in Colorado.

Black-tailed
Jackrabbit

AMERICAN PIKA
Ochotona princeps
Size: To 9 in. (23 cm)

Description: A small, roundish mammal with short legs and dark ears. Fur is brown above and light below.

Habitat: Talus slopes and rocky fields near the timberline.

Comments: It can be seen scurrying about rock piles gathering vegetation that it stores to feed on during winter months. Lives in small colonies. Sharp, shrill squeaks are a familiar sound in alpine areas. Active year-round.

SQUIRRELS & ALLIES

This diverse family of hairy-tailed, large-eyed rodents includes chipmunks, tree squirrels, ground squirrels and marmots. Most are active during the day and are easily observed in the field. Note that size includes tail length.

GOLDEN-MANTLED GROUND SQUIRREL
Spermophilus lateralis
Size: 9–12 in. (23–30 cm)

Description: Told by its coppery head and shoulders and long white side stripe bordered in black. Unlike similar-looking chipmunks, it lacks facial stripes.

Habitat: Moist coniferous forests in the mountains.

Comments: When predators approach, individuals will sound warning calls causing all to flee to the safety of their burrows. Those found near campgrounds are often very tame.

ROCK SQUIRREL
Otospermophilus variegatus
Size: 17–21 in. (43–53 cm)
Description: Large mottled grayish ground squirrel with a long, bushy tail.
Habitat: Rocky canyons and slopes.
Comments: Often seen sitting on rocks watching for danger. Unlike many ground-dwelling squirrels, it climbs trees easily.

THIRTEEN-LINED GROUND SQUIRREL
Spermophilus tridecemlineatus
Size: 7–12 in. (18–30 cm)
Description: Brownish rodent has 13 alternating brown and white lines on its back and sides.
Habitat: Prairies, along roadsides, yards, golf courses.
Comments: Active during the day, it can be observed feeding and ducking in and out of its numerous burrows. Feeds primarily on plants and invertebrates.

WYOMING GROUND SQUIRREL
Spermophilus elegans
Size: To 11 in. (28 cm)
Description: Yellow-gray squirrel has a black-tipped tail edged in cream.
Habitat: Grasslands, meadows, montane regions, talus slopes in northwestern Colorado.
Comments: Makes cricket-like chirps when near burrow entrance. Most active at dawn and dusk.

COLORADO CHIPMUNK
Tamias quadrivittatus
Size: 8–10 in. (20–25 cm)
Description: Small rodent has red-brown fur. Key field marks are dark and light stripes on its face.
Habitat: Desert scrub, grasslands, coniferous forests.
Comments: Colorado is home to five species of chipmunks, all of which have striped faces and look very similar. Browsing signs include piles of nut and acorn shells.

RED SQUIRREL
Tamiasciurus hudsonicus
Size: 11–15 in. (28–38 cm)

Description: Rusty-olive squirrel has a whitish belly and underparts. Bushy tail is orangish.

Habitat: Mixed, hardwood and coniferous forests.

Comments: Active during the day, it is very vocal and often heard twittering and chattering. Feeds on seeds, berries and nuts. Spends much of the summer caching winter food stores.

ABERT'S SQUIRREL
Sciurus aberti
Size: 17–23 in. (43–58 cm)

Description: Large squirrel has pronounced tufts of hair on its ears. Coat is grayish, black or brown.

Habitat: Coniferous forests in central and southwestern Colorado.

Comments: Locally common squirrel feeds primarily on the seed cones, inner bark and buds of the ponderosa pine. It is estimated 65% of the Colorado population are black-colored. Active year-round.

BLACK-TAILED PRAIRIE DOG
Cynomys ludovicianus
Size: 12–16 in. (30–40 cm)

Description: Chunky rodent has a short, black-tipped tail. Presence is detected by bare mounds of earth with numerous burrow openings.

Habitat: Shortgrass prairies in eastern Colorado.

Comments: Lives in large colonies called prairie dog towns that can have up to several thousand individuals. Active during the day, it is easily observed. Considered a "keystone" species because their colonies create islands of habitat that benefit other species. Noted for their habit of touching noses and incisors when they greet each other that looks like kissing. The similar white-tailed prairie dog (*C. leucurus*) is found in northeastern Colorado, and the Gunnison's prairie dog (*C. gunnisoni*) is found in southwestern Colorado.

WHITE-TAILED ANTELOPE SQUIRREL
Ammospermophilus leucurus

Size: 8–10 in. (20–25 cm)

Description: Brownish rodent has a white tail trimmed in black that it holds aloft.

Habitat: Foothills and deserts in eastern Colorado.

Comments: Holds tail aloft while running, using it as an umbrella to shade the sun. Active throughout the day.

YELLOW-BELLIED MARMOT
Marmota flaviventris

Size: 18–28 in. (45–70 cm)

Description: Large, yellow-brown rodent with a yellow belly. Many have a white patch between the eyes.

Habitat: Rocky alpine areas above 5,000 ft. (1800 m).

Comments: Primarily diurnal, it is often seen foraging and sunbathing. Calls include a whistling, highly-pitched chirp, a scream and a tooth chatter. Also called rock chuck and whistle-pig, it lives in colonies. Hibernates from September to May.

POCKET GOPHERS

These mole-like mammals are known for the mounds of dirt they push up when excavating their burrows. They are named for their fur-lined, external cheek pouches that they stuff with food or nesting material.

NORTHERN POCKET GOPHER
Thomomys talpoides

Size: 6–10 in. (15–25 cm)

Description: A small, roundish mammal with short legs and dark ears. Fur is brown above and light below. Has prominent, crescent-shaped claws.

Habitat: Areas with soft soil.

Comments: Feeds underground by chewing off the stems of plants below the surface and pulling them into the burrow.

MICE & ALLIES

Most members of this large group have large ears, long tails and breed throughout the year. Dedicated omnivores, they have adapted to practically every North American habitat. Sizes noted include tail length.

DEER MOUSE
Peromyscus maniculatus
Size: 4–8 in. (10–20 cm)
Description: Bicolored coat is pale gray to red-brown above and white below. Tail is hairy.
Habitat: Common and widespread in diverse habitats.
Comments: Feeds on a variety of foods including seeds, buds, fruit and invertebrates. Active year-round.

HOUSE MOUSE
Mus musculus
Size: 5–8 in. (13–20 cm)
Description: Told by its gray coat, large eyes and ears and scaly tail.
Habitat: Agricultural areas, near human dwellings.
Comments: Normally lives in underground burrows but easily adapts to crevices in buildings. Females have up to 5 litters of 4–8 young annually. Eats grain, seeds, insects and garbage.

NORWAY RAT
Rattus norvegicus
Size: 12–18 in. (30–45 cm)
Description: Large gray-brown rodent with a scaly tail.
Habitat: Common in urban areas, sewers, marshes and grain fields.
Comments: One of the most destructive and widespread pests, it eats food, garbage and damages structures and spreads disease. Albino strains of this species are commonly used in lab experiments and have greatly helped the advancement of medicine and science.

ORD'S KANGAROO RAT
Dipodomys ordii
Size: 8–11 in. (20–28 cm)
Description: Distinguished by its large hind feet and long tail. Coat is buff above, white below.
Habitat: Open areas with sandy soils.
Comments: Capable of leaping up to 8 ft. (1.8–2.4 m) in a single bound. Active year-round, it feeds on the seeds of mesquite, sunflowers and other plants.

WESTERN JUMPING MOUSE
Zapus princeps
Size: 8–10 in. (20–25 cm)
Description: Coat is olive above, yellowish on the sides and white below. Large hind legs and long tail assist it in bounding across the ground.
Habitat: Found in mountain meadows and open woodlands near water.
Comments: Capable of leaping up to 6 ft. (1.8 m).

SOUTHERN RED-BACKED VOLE
Clethrionomys gapperi
Size: To 6 in. (15 cm)
Description: Fuzzy, mouse-like rodent has gray-brown sides and a reddish back.
Habitat: Damp forests and meadows.
Comments: Often scurries about under ground cover and is difficult to observe. Active throughout the year, it tunnels through the snow in winter. One of 8 species of vole found in Colorado.

BUSHY-TAILED WOODRAT
Neotoma cinerea
Size: 12–18 in. (30–45 cm)
Description: Brown to grayish rodent has a bushy, squirrel-like tail.
Habitat: Brushy areas of foothills and deserts.
Comments: Also called pack rat, it often builds large houses of sticks that it uses to cache vegetation and shiny objects it steals from hikers.

PORCUPINES

Porcupines are medium-sized mammals with coats of stiff, barbed quills. When threatened, it faces away from its aggressor, erects its quills and lashes out with its tail. The loosely rooted quills detach on contact and are extremely difficult to remove.

COMMON PORCUPINE
Erethizon dorsatum

Size: 25–37 in. (63–93 cm)
Description: Told by its chunky profile, arched back and long gray coat of barbed quills.
Habitat: Forested areas.
Comments: Spends much of its time in trees feeding on leaves, twigs and bark. Signs include unique tracks and trees that have large patches of bark removed.

RACCOONS & ALLIES

All members of this diverse family of omnivorous mammals have ringed tails.

COMMON RACCOON
Procyon lotor

Size: To 3 ft. (90 cm)
Description: Easily distinguished by its black mask and ringed tail.
Habitat: Forests, thickets and farmlands statewide up to 8,000 ft. (2400 m).
Comments: Rests during the day and feeds on small animals, insects, invertebrates and garbage at night. Often dunks its food into water before eating it. Unique hand-like tracks are commonly seen in streamside mud.

RINGTAIL
Bassariscus astutus

Size: 24–32 in. (60–80 cm)
Description: Has large eyes, large ears and a long, ringed tail. Lacks a black mask.
Habitat: Rocky areas, rough country, chaparral.
Comments: Hunts at night, killing prey with a bite to the neck. Nicknamed Miners' Cats, they were once used like cats to control rodent populations in mines.

SKUNKS, WEASELS & ALLIES

Members of this group usually have small heads, long necks, short legs and long bodies. All but sea otters have prominent anal scent glands that are used for social and sexual communication.

AMERICAN BADGER
Taxidea taxus

Size: 20–34 in. (50–85 cm)

Description: A squat, heavy-bodied animal with a long yellow-gray to brown coat, white forehead stripe and long foreclaws.

Habitat: Grasslands and uncultivated pastures, deserts.

Comments: A prodigious burrower that feeds mostly on burrowing mammals, other rodents and ground-dwelling birds.

LONG-TAILED WEASEL
Mustela frenata

Size: 13–22 in. (33–55 cm)

Description: Told by slender body and long, black-tipped tail. Summer coat is brown above, whitish to yellowish below. Feet are brownish. Those found above 4,000 ft. (1220 m) have a winter coat that is all white except for the black tip on tail.

Habitat: Found near water in open woodlands, meadows and fields statewide.

Comments: Weasels are aggressive hunters and are notorious for killing more prey than they can eat.

SHORT-TAILED WEASEL
Mustela erminea

Size: To 14 in. (35 cm)

Description: Long-bodied mammal has short legs, a medium length, black-tipped tail and whitish to yellowish feet. Coat is brown above and white below in summer and all-white in winter.

Habitat: Forested areas above 8,000 ft. (2400 m).

Comments. Also called ermine, it eats small animal prey. Swims and climbs well.

MINK
Neovison vison
Size: To 28 in. (70 cm)
Description: Told by rich brown coat, it often has white spotting on its chin and throat.
Habitat: Common near water in a variety of habitats.
Comments: Highly aquatic, it builds dens along river and stream banks and feeds on fish, amphibians, crustaceans and small mammals.

NORTHERN RIVER OTTER
Lontra canadensis
Size: 40–52 in. (1–1.3 m)
Description: Sleek, long-bodied mammal has a glossy, gray-brown coat, thick tail and webbed hind feet.
Habitat: Lakes and rivers.
Comments: Hunts on land and in fresh- and saltwater where it feeds on fishes, amphibians, crustaceans and small mammals. Endangered in Colorado, it is being reintroduced around the state.

STRIPED SKUNK
Mephitis mephitis
Size: To 30 in. (75 cm)
Description: Distinguished by its black coat, white forehead stripe and white side stripes.
Habitat: Open wooded areas near water, farmland and suburbs statewide.
Comments: Protects itself by spraying aggressors with noxious smelling fluids from its anal glands. Spray is effective up to 15 ft. (5 m) away. Feeds at night, primarily on vegetation, insects and small mammals.

Threat display

WESTERN SPOTTED SKUNK
Spilogale gracilis
Size: 9–19 in. (23–48 cm)
Description: Black coat has 4–6 irregular stripes. White spots on head and sides.
Habitat: Mixed woodlands, wastelands.
Comments: When threatened, it gives warning by raising its tail, doing a handstand and spreading its hind feet before spraying. A good climber and swimmer, it often preys on birds and their eggs.

BEAVERS & MUSKRATS

Found on rivers, lakes and marshes, beavers are the largest North American rodents. Highly aquatic, they have webbed feet and long, broad tails that they slap on the water's surface when alarmed.

AMERICAN BEAVER
Castor canadensis
Size: 40–48 in. (1–1.2 m)
Description: Told by glossy brown coat and flattened, scaly tail.
Habitat: Lakes, ponds and streams from 4,000 ft. (1200 m) to the timberline.
Comments: Many beavers live in dens excavated along stream banks; others build cone-shaped houses (lodges) of sticks and mud in deep water and will even dam a waterway to create a suitable pond. Diet consists of the bark of deciduous trees and shrubs (aspens, willows, maples), leaves, buds, forbs and sedges.

COMMON MUSKRAT
Ondatra zibethicus
Size: To 2 ft. (60 cm)
Description: Often mistaken for beavers, these aquatic rodents are smaller and have a long scaly tail that is flattened on either side.
Habitat: Marshes, lakes, waterways.
Comments: In swampy areas, they construct dome-shaped houses of marsh vegetation up to 3 ft. (90 cm) high. Feeds primarily on aquatic plants. Active year-round.

DOG-LIKE MAMMALS

Members of this family have long snouts, erect ears and resemble domestic dogs in looks and habit. All are active year-round.

COYOTE
Canis latrans
Size: To 52 in. (1.3 m)
Description: Yellow-gray with a pointed nose, rusty legs and ears and a bushy, black-tipped tail.
Habitat: Wooded and open areas throughout Colorado.
Comments: Largely a nocturnal hunter, it is often seen loping across fields at dawn and dusk. Holds its tail down when running. Feeds on rodents, rabbits, berries and carrion.

COMMON GRAY FOX
Urocyon cinereoargenteus

Size: 30–48 in. (75–120 cm)
Description: Distinguished by its coat, which is brownish-gray above and rusty-white below.
Habitat: Deciduous woodlands, forests.
Comments: Primarily nocturnal, it is occasionally spotted foraging during the day. An excellent climber, it often seeks refuge in trees.

RED FOX
Vulpes vulpes

Size: 35–45 in. (88–114 cm)
Description: Small, rusty-reddish fox has a bushy, white-tipped tail and dark stockings. Silver, black and red-silver variants also exist.
Habitat: Mixed woodlands, brushy areas, forest edges statewide.
Comments: Feeds on small animals, birds, insects, fruits, carrion and garbage. Primarily nocturnal.

CAT-LIKE MAMMALS

These highly specialized carnivores are renowned hunters. All have short faces, keen vision, powerful bodies and retractable claws. Most are nocturnal hunters.

BOBCAT
Lynx rufus

Size: To 4 ft. (1.2 m)
Description: Key field marks are its spotted red-brown coat, short tail and tufted ears.
Habitat: Scrubby open woodlands, thickets, swamps. Found throughout Colorado at elevations below 10,000 ft. (3000 m).
Comments: Named for its bobbed tail, it rests in thickets by day and hunts rabbits and rodents by night.

MOUNTAIN LION
Puma concolor

Size: 5–9 ft. (1.5–2.7 m)
Description: Large tan cat has a whitish belly and long, black-tipped tail.
Habitat: Rocky canyons, forests, foothills.
Comments: A solitary hunter, it hunts hoofed mammals, hares and other small mammals at night. Also called cougar and puma, it weighs up to 200 lbs. (91 kg).

BEARS

This group includes the largest terrestrial carnivores in the world. All are heavy-bodied, large-headed animals, with short ears and small tails. Their sense of smell is keen, although their eyesight is generally poor.

BLACK BEAR
Ursus americanus
Size: 4–6 ft. (1.2–1.8 m)

Description: Coat is normally black, but cinnamon, dark brown and blond variants also occur. Snout is straight and muzzle is brown. Many black bears in Colorado are some shade of brown.

Habitat: Primarily forested areas in central and western Colorado.

Comments: Diet is 95% vegetarian and consists of berries, acorns, grasses and forbs. Animal matter in its diet is made up of insects, small animals and carrion. Signs include tracks, scat and scratched trees. In cold weather, resting/hibernating bears can be detected by the steam from their breath at den openings.

HOOFED MAMMALS

This general grouping includes odd- and even-toed hoofed mammals from a variety of families.

BIGHORN SHEEP
Ovis canadensis
Size: 5–6 ft. (1.5–1.8 m)

Description: Gray to brownish, males are easily distinguished by their massive coiled horns. Females have small, nearly upright horns.

Habitat: Mountainous areas above 8,000 ft. (2400 m).

Comments: Males and females form separate herds for most of the year. Horns are never shed. Rams weigh up to 350 lbs. (160 kg) and battle for females in November by bashing their horns together.

Colorado's State Animal

MOUNTAIN GOAT
Oreamnos americanus
Size: To 6 ft. (1.8 m)

Description: Distinguished by its long, shaggy white coat and black, upright, dagger-like horns (both sexes).

Habitat: Remote mountainous areas.

Comments: Found in high alpine meadows in summer and near the treeline in winter. Powerful climbers, they have specialized 'suction-cup' hooves that enhance their traction on rocky slopes. Has been introduced in several Colorado parks since 1017.

MULE DEER
Odocoileus hemionus

Size: 4–8 ft. (1.2–2.4 m)

Description: Distinguished by its large 'mule-sized' ears and black-tipped tail. Antlers of mature bucks branch from the main beam and each tine branches again.

Habitat: Open habitats where forest and shrublands mingle with meadows. Lives at higher elevations in the summer.

Comments: Feeds mostly on shrubs, twigs and grasses. Males shed antlers January–March. The most common large mammal in the state, Colorado is estimated to be home to 400,000 deer.

WHITE-TAILED DEER
Odocoileus virginianus

Size: 6–7 ft. (1.8–2.1 m)

Description: Coat is tan in summer, grayish in winter. Named for its large, white-edged tail that is held aloft, flag-like, when running. Antlers of mature white-tailed bucks have one main beam; the tines do not branch.

Habitat: Forests, farmlands and river valleys in eastern and northwestern Colorado.

Comments: An agile, elusive deer, it can reach speeds of 40 mph (65 kph) and leap obstacles as high as 8 ft. (2.5 m). Most active at dawn and dusk.

PRONGHORN
Antilocapra americana

Size: 4–5 ft. (1.2–1.5 m)

Description: A tan, deer-like animal with white throat bands and a white rump. Males have stumpy, pronged horns. Females have short, single horns.

Habitat: Open grasslands and sagebrush flats.

Comments: Active during the night or day. The fastest animal in North America, it has been clocked at speeds up to 84 mph (135 kph).

ELK
Cervus canadensis
Size: 6–9 ft. (1.8–2.7 m)

Description: Large deer with shaggy brown neck and light rump patch. Coat is brownish in winter and lighter in summer.

Habitat: Meadows and forested areas.

Comments: Primarily nocturnal, it is also active at dusk and dawn and travels in large herds. Moves up to mountain meadows to feed during the summer and returns to lower elevation forests in winter. During the fall breeding season males fight for the females and often bugle loudly during rutting season. Males shed antlers annually. Colorado boasts the largest elk population – 260,000 animals – of any state or province in North America.

AMERICAN BISON
Bos bison
Size: To 12 ft. (3.6 m)

Description: Easily distinguished by its shaggy mane and massive forequarters.

Habitat: Grasslands, plains, woodlands.

Comments: Herds of bison can be seen at Rocky Mountain Arsenal National Wildlife Refuge just outside of Denver, Genesee Park and Soapstone Prairie Natural Area.

MOOSE
Alces alces
Size: To 9 ft. (2.7 m)

Description: Huge animal has long, thin legs and a pendulous snout. Males have enormous, flattened antlers and a prominent neck 'bell' of skin and hair.

Habitat: Forests near shallow lakes, rivers and swamps in northwestern Colorado.

Comments: Largely solitary animals, they are most active at dawn and dusk. Females with young can be very aggressive and should be avoided at all costs. Considered a non-resident species in Colorado until new populations were successfully re-introduced in 1978–79.

Birds are warm-blooded, feathered animals with two wings and two legs. The majority can fly and those that cannot are believed to be descended from ancestors that did. Adaptations for flight include hollow bones and an enhanced breathing capacity. Birds also have an efficient four-chambered heart and are insulated against the weather to help temperature regulation.

How to Identify Birds

As with other species, the best way to become good at identifying birds is to practice. The more birds you try to identify, the better you will become at distinguishing species.

When birding, the first thing to note is the habitat you are exploring in order to know what kinds of birds to expect. When you spot a bird, check for obvious field marks. Note the shape of its silhouette and beak. Note the color and pattern of its feathers for distinguishing markings at rest and in flight. Is it small (sparrow), medium (crow), or large (heron)? Does it have any unusual behavioral characteristics?

If you are interested in enhancing your field skills, it is essential to become familiar with bird songs since many species that are difficult to observe in the field are readily identified by their distinctive song. Bird song apps and CDs are available online and from nature stores and libraries.

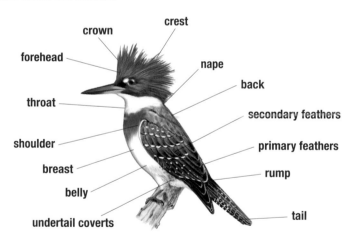

N.B. – It is important to note that most species illustrations in this guide feature the adult male in its breeding coloration. Colors and markings shown may be duller or absent during different times of the year.

GREBES

The members of this group of duck-like birds have short tails, slender necks and stiff bills. Excellent divers, they have lobed toes rather than webbed feet and have legs located near the back of the body to help propel them through the water.

PIED-BILLED GREBE
Podilymbus podiceps

Size: 12–15 in. (30–38 cm)

Description: Distinguished by its small size and chicken-like white bill. Breeding birds have a black-banded bill and black throat. Non-breeding adults are grayish.

Habitat: Freshwater ponds, lakes and weed-choked marshes.

Comments: Often swims with body partially submerged. Hatchlings are often carried and fed on the backs of their parents.

WESTERN GREBE
Aechmophorus occidentalis

Size: 20–29 in. (50–73 cm)

Description: Long-necked, slender-billed bird is black above, white below.

Habitat: Large lakes and coastal waters.

Comments: Winters along the coast in large numbers. Noted for their spectacular courtship display in which two birds "rush" side-by-side and run across the water's surface in pairs.

GEESE

Geese are large, long-necked birds found near ponds and marshes. Highly terrestrial, they are often spotted grazing in fields and meadows. Their diet consists largely of grasses, grains and some aquatic plants. Noisy in flight, they are often heard before they're seen passing overhead.

CANADA GOOSE
Branta canadensis

Size: 24–45 in. (60–114 cm)

Description: Told by black head and neck, and white cheek patch.

Habitat: Marshes, ponds, lakes, rivers, parks, golf courses, agricultural fields.

Comments: Geese fly in a V-formation when migrating. Pairs usually mate for life. Call is a nasal – *honk*. Geese feed on plants, grains, grass, insects, crustaceans and other invertebrates. Like dabbling ducks, they tip-up to feed in shallow waters. Thousands overwinter on Denver area golf courses.

DUCKS & ALLIES

Smaller than geese, ducks have shorter necks and are primarily aquatic. In most, breeding males are more brightly colored than females. Both sexes have a brightly colored band (speculum) on the trailing edge of the wing.

WOOD DUCK
Aix sponsa
Size: To 20 in. (50 cm)

Description: Multi-colored, crested male has a green head, white neck, red eyes and red bill. Female is dull-colored with a white eye patch.

Habitat: Wooded ponds, marshes, lakes, rivers.

Comments: Often seen perching in trees, it is one of a few ducks to nest in tree cavities. Found in forested wetlands, along rivers and swamps. Female makes loud – *oo-eek, oo-eek* – when disturbed and taking flight.

RUDDY DUCK
Oxyura jamaicensis
Size: 15–16 in. (38–40 cm)

Description: Note its sloping profile, thick neck, broad bill and white cheeks.

Habitat: Lakes, ponds, rivers.

Comments: Tail is often cocked in the air when swimming.

MALLARD
Anas platyrhynchos
Size: 20–28 in. (50–70 cm)

Description: Male has a green head, white collar and chestnut breast. Female is mottled brown. Both have a metallic blue speculum.

Habitat: Ponds and marshes.

Comments: The ancestor of domestic ducks, it is the most numerous and widespread nesting duck in Colorado. Hundreds of thousands also winter here. Call is a loud – *quack*.

GREEN-WINGED TEAL
Anas crecca
Size: 12–16 in. (30–40 cm)

Description: Male has chestnut colored head and a green eye patch. Female is brown-gray with a green speculum.

Habitat: Lakes and ponds.

Comments: Fast fliers that travel in tight flocks. Females weigh as little as 5 oz. (140 g).

RING-NECKED DUCK
Aythya collaris
Size: To 18 in. (45 cm)

Description: Male has a ringed bill, dark head and back and a vertical white side stripe. Mottled female has a similar bill and a light eye ring.

Habitat: Wooded lakes, ponds, marshes.

Comments: Often occurs in pairs or small flocks. Dives to feed on insects, mollusks, invertebrates and vegetation.

NORTHERN SHOVELER
Spatula clypeata
Size: 17–20 in. (43–50 cm)

Description: Told by its flat head and large, spatulate bill. Male has a green head, rusty sides and a blue wing patch.

Habitat: Marshes, lakes, ponds.

Comments: Large, shovel-shaped bill has comb-like projections on its edges that allow it to strain aquatic animals and vegetation from the water. Swims with bill pointed downward.

NORTHERN PINTAIL
Anas acuta
Size: 20–30 in. (50–75 cm)

Description: Distinguished by its long neck and pointed tail. Male has a brown head and a white breast and neck stripe. Both sexes have a glossy brown speculum that is bordered in white.

Habitat: Shallow marshes and ponds.

Comments: Call is a short whistle. Begins nesting as soon as ice thaws in spring.

GADWALL
Mareca strepera
Size: To 21 in. (53 cm)

Description: Male has a gray body and black rump. Both sexes have a white belly and a white patch on the hind edge of the wing.

Habitat: Freshwater ponds, marshes, rivers.

Comments: A dabbling duck, it feeds by tipping over so that its tail sticks up in the air. Call is a raspy *nheh.*

COMMON MERGANSER
Mergus merganser
Size: 22–27 in. (55–68 cm)

Description: Told by sleek profile and long, slender, serrated bill. Male has an iridescent black-green head and white underparts. Female has a crested rufous head and a sharply defined white throat.

Habitat: Wooded lakes and rivers.

Comments: A diving duck, it feeds primarily on fish. Also called sawbills, fish ducks or goosanders.

BLUE-WINGED TEAL
Anas discors
Size: 15–16 in. (38–40 cm)

Description: Male's white facial crescent is distinctive. Female has spotted sides. Note blue forewing in flight.

Habitat: Ponds, marshes, estuaries.

Comments: Has been known to migrate over 4,000 miles (6440 km) to its wintering grounds in South America.

AMERICAN WIGEON
Mareca americana
Size: 18–23 in. (45–58 cm)

Description: Male is brownish with a gray head and a glossy green face patch. Female has a bluish bill and flecked head. Speculum is green.

Habitat: Freshwater streams, lakes, marshes.

Comments: Though primarily aquatic, these ducks can often be found nibbling grass on the shores of ponds and marshes. Male's call sounds like a squeaky toy. Female gives a harsh quack. Also known as baldpate.

REDHEAD
Aythya americana
Size: To 22 in. (55 cm)

Description: Note rounded, cinnamon head. Female has a light eye ring. Summers on inland lakes and ponds, and winters in warmer areas along the coast.

Habitat: Open lakes, prairie ponds.

Comments: Feeds mostly at night, resting on the water during daylight. Often found in huge flocks. Females often lay their eggs in the nests of other birds.

CINNAMON TEAL
Spatula cyanoptera
Size: 14–17 in. (35–43 cm)
Description: Both sexes have a chalky blue forewing patch. Males are bright cinnamon; females are mottled brown.
Habitat: Marshes, shallow ponds and rivers.
Comments: The forewing patches are most visible in flight.

BUFFLEHEAD
Bucephala albeola
Size: To 15 in. (38 cm)
Description: Small, puffy-headed duck. Male is distinguished by the large white patch on its iridescent, black head. Female is gray-brown with a white cheek patch.
Habitat: Lakes, estuaries, rivers in winter.
Comments: A diving duck, it feeds on fishes, crustaceans and mollusks.

COMMON GOLDENEYE
Bucephala clangula
Size: To 20 in. (50 cm)
Description: Male is distinguished by its glossy green head and white patch below its eye. Mottled gray female has a tawny head.
Habitat: Large lakes and rivers in winter.
Comments: Also known as "whistler" by hunters for the sound its wings make in flight. Nests in tree cavities.

COOTS

Coots are chicken-billed birds often found in the company of ducks and geese. They are, however, more closely related to cranes than to ducks.

AMERICAN COOT
Fulica americana
Size: 13–16 in. (33–40 cm)
Description: Dark bird has a chicken-like white bill, white rump and long greenish legs.
Habitat: Lakes, ponds and marshes.
Comments: Feeds on the shore and in the wate Habitually pumps its head back and forth when swimming. Unlike ducks, they have lobed rather than webbed feet.

WADING BIRDS, SHOREBIRDS & ALLIES

This general category includes several diverse families of birds that are typically found along shorelines on or near water.

BLACK-NECKED STILT
Himantopus mexicanus
Size: 12–16 in. (30–40 cm)
Description: Slender black and white wader has a thin bill and long, rose-pink legs.
Habitat: Wetlands, mudflats.
Comments: A highly vocal bird, it emits loud, yapping calls when disturbed or threatened.

GREAT BLUE HERON
Ardea herodias
Size: 40–52 in. (1–1.3 m)
Description: Large, slender grayish-blue bird has long legs, a long, yellowish bill and white face. Black plumes extend back from the eye.
Habitat: Wetlands, margins of ponds, lakes and waterways below 8,000 ft. (2400 m).
Comments: Often seen stalking fish and frogs in shallow water. Flies with its neck tucked in and long legs trailing behind. Despite their large size, adults only weigh about 5 lbs. (2.2 kg). Chatfield Reservoir is a prime nesting site for hundreds of birds.

BLACK-CROWNED NIGHT-HERON
Nycticorax nycticorax
Size: To 28 in. (70 cm)
Description: Distinguished by black crown and back, gray sides and tail and white underparts.
Habitat: Wetlands in eastern Colorado.
Comments: Feeds at dusk, dawn and during the night along waterways stalking fish, amphibians and small reptiles and mammals. Common along the South Platte River.

WHITE-FACED IBIS
Plegadis chihi
Size: 22–25 in. (55–63 cm)
Description: Dark wading bird has a long, thin, downcurved bill.
Habitat: Wetlands.
Comments: Feeds on insects, amphibians, fishes, shellfish and crustaceans.

GREAT EGRET
Ardea alba
Size: To 40 in. (1 m)

SNOWY EGRET
Egretta thula
Size: To 27 in. (68 cm)
Description: Slender white wading birds. Great egret has a yellow bill and black feet. The smaller snowy egret has a black bill and yellow feet.
Habitat: Marshes, lakes, estuaries.
Comments: Usually feeds by stalking prey in shallow water. The only other similar large white wading bird is the white morph of the great blue heron. It has yellow legs and a yellow bill.

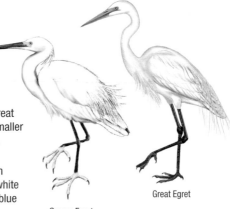
Great Egret

Snowy Egret

AMERICAN AVOCET
Recurvirostra americana
Size: 15–20 in. (38–50 cm)
Description: Large shorebird has long legs and a long upcurved bill. Breeding birds have a tawny head and neck.
Habitat: Shallow ponds, marshes, mudflats.
Comments: Feeds by working bill side to side while walking head down through the water.

SANDHILL CRANE
Grus canadensis
Size: To 4 ft. (1.2 m)
Description: Long-legged, gray wading bird has a red forecrown and white cheeks.
Habitat: Open wetlands, fields, prairies.
Comments: Unlike herons, it flies with its neck outstretched. Cranes communicate with each other via a series of complicated gestures and dances. Up to 500,000 birds migrate through the Platte River area of Nebraska each spring. Tens of thousands migrate through Colorado each spring and fall. A small number breed in areas of northwestern Colorado including Yampa River and ponds in Routt and Jackson counties.

DOUBLE-CRESTED CORMORANT
Phalacrocorax auritus
Size: 30–36 in. (75–90 cm)

Description: Glossy black bird has a slender neck, hooked bill and red throat pouch.

Habitat: Large lakes and rivers.

Comments: Nests in colonies and is often seen perched on trees and pilings near marinas. Often perches with wings outstretched to allow them to dry. Swims low in water when diving for fish.

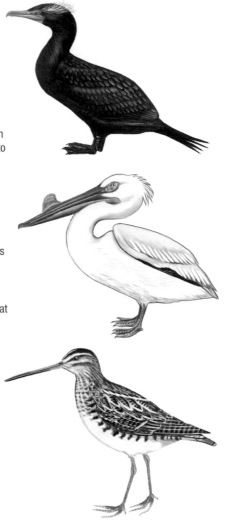

AMERICAN WHITE PELICAN
Pelecanus erythrorhynchos
Size: To 6 ft. (1.8 m)

Description: Large, stout white bird has a long bill and an orange-yellow throat pouch. Wing tips are black.

Habitat: Large lakes.

Comments: Often travels in flocks that fly in a V-formation. Feeds by scooping fish into its throat pouch. Migrates south from Colorado in fall.

WILSON'S SNIPE
Gallinago delicata
Size: 10–12 in. (25–30 cm)

Description: Stocky bird has a very long bill, striped head and heavily barred sides and flanks.

Habitat: Wet meadows, marshes and muddy fields.

Comments: Noted for their elaborate breeding display in which males make spectacular swooping flights and a haunting sound (winnowing) created by air flowing over its tail feathers.

SPOTTED SANDPIPER
Actitis macularius
Size: 6–8 in. (15–20 cm)

Description: Small brown bird has light, dark-spotted underparts and spindly, yellowish legs. Spots are evident during breeding season.

Habitat: Near water with vegetated shorelines.

Comments: A solitary bird, it teeters back and forth when walking. Flies with quivering wings held downward, alternating with low glides.

KILLDEER
Charadrius vociferus
Size: 9–11 in. (23–28 cm)
Description: Brown bird has a white breast and two black neck bands.
Habitat: Open areas near water in urban and rural settings.
Comments: Shrill call – *kill-dee, kill-dee* – is repeated continuously. Adults will often feign injury to lead intruders away from their nesting area.

GULLS & ALLIES

These long-winged birds are strong fliers and excellent swimmers. Gulls are usually gray and white and have webbed feet and square tails; immature birds are brownish.

RING-BILLED GULL
Larus delawarensis
Size: To 20 in. (50 cm)
Description: Key field marks are a black-ringed bill, yellow eyes, yellow legs and a dark-tipped white tail.
Habitat: Found near lakes, rivers, fields, waste dumps and shopping malls.
Comments: Varied diet includes carrion, garbage, eggs, young birds and aquatic animals.

HERRING GULL
Larus argentatus smithsonianus
Size: To 26 in. (65 cm)
Description: Key field marks are white-spotted, black wing tips, yellow eyes and pink legs.
Habitat: Lakes, rivers, garbage dumps.
Comments: The largest gull that is common inland, it is a winter resident in eastern Colorado.

CALIFORNIA GULL
Larus californicus
Size: 20–23 in. (50–58 cm)
Description: Told by its gray back, white-spotted black wing tips and greenish legs. Bill has a red spot on the lower mandible.
Habitat: Inland lakes and ponds during breeding season, coastal shorelines in winter.
Comments: Highly social, they breed in colonies. Typically forage in open areas including farms, pastures and garbage dumps.

BIRDS OF PREY

Primarily carnivorous, these birds have sharp talons for grasping prey and sharply hooked bills for tearing into flesh. Many soar on wind currents when hunting. Genders are similar in most.

TURKEY VULTURE
Cathartes aura
Size: 26–32 in. (65–80 cm)
Description: Large, brown-black bird has a naked red head. Trailing half of wings are silvery.
Habitat: Dry, open country statewide.
Comments: Glides with its wings held in a slight "V" as it wheels about the sky searching for carrion.

RED-TAILED HAWK
Buteo jamaicensis
Size: 20–25 in. (50–63 cm)
Description: Dark, broad-winged, wide-tailed hawk has light underparts that are darkly streaked and a reddish tail.
Habitat: Open fields and forests, farmlands.
Comments: This familiar hawk is often spotted perched on roadside poles and fence posts.

OSPREY
Pandion haliaetus
Size: 20–25 in. (50–63 cm)
Description: Large raptor has a dark brown back, light underparts and a dark eye stripe.
Habitat: Coastal, inland lakes and rivers.
Comments: Unlike most soaring birds, it glides with its wings arched. Often hovers over the water before diving after fish. Its unusual talons allow it to grasp prey with two toes in front and two behind.

GOLDEN EAGLE
Aquila chrysaetos
Size: 30–41 in. (75–104 cm)
Description: Large, dark brown raptor has a tawny wash on its head and neck. Dark tail is finely barred.
Habitat: Mountain regions, hilly terrain.
Comments: Feeds on mammals, birds and carrion. Often builds nests on power poles. Wingspan is up to 7.5 ft. (2.3 m).

BALD EAGLE
Haliaeetus leucocephalus
Size: 30–43 in. (75–109 cm)

Description: Large dark bird has a white head, neck and tail. Legs and bill are yellow.

Habitat: Near lakes and rivers where fish are abundant.

Comments: Feeds on fish and waterbirds. Distinctive plumage is not attained for several years; young birds are brown and easily confused with golden eagles.

Juvenile

AMERICAN KESTREL
Falco sparverius
Size: 9–12 in. (23–30 cm)

Description: Small falcon has a rust back and tail and pointed, narrow, spotted blue wings. Male has black facial marks.

Habitat: A variety of open habitats in urban and rural settings.

Comments: Formerly called the sparrow hawk. Often pumps its tail when perching.

NORTHERN HARRIER
Circus hudsonius
Size: 18–24 in. (45–60 cm)

Description: Slim hawk is gray above and light below with chestnut spotting on breast. Note long tail and V-shaped flight profile. White rump is conspicuous in flight.

Habitat: Marshes, grasslands.

Comments: Flies a few feet above the ground, wavering from side to side as it hunts rodents and other small prey.

PRAIRIE FALCON
Falco mexicanus
Size: 16–20 in. (40–50 cm)

Description: Plumage is pale brown above and white and spotted below. Note facial markings. Dark "armpits" are visible in flight.

Habitat: Dry, open areas.

Comments: Feeds primarily on small mammals and birds. A year-round resident throughout most of Colorado.

SHARP-SHINNED HAWK
Accipiter striatus

Size: 12–14 in. (30–35 cm)

Description: Plumage is gray above and light below. Underparts are barred with brownish-orange stripes. Females tend to be browner than males.

Habitat: Forests.

Comments: The sharp-shinned hawk has short, rounded wings that enable it to maneuver through dense woods in search of prey.

COOPER'S HAWK
Accipiter cooperii

Size: 14–20 in. (35–50 cm)

Description: Distinguished from the smaller sharp-shinned hawk by its size and rounded head.

Habitat: Mixed woodlands.

Comments: These birds are common in urban areas and feed primarily on songbirds and small animals.

FERRUGINOUS HAWK
Buteo regalis

Size: To 27 in. (68 cm)

Description: Large red-brown hawk has a white, unbanded tail. Light morphs have rusty legs that form a "V" under the light tail in flight. The rare dark morphs have all-brown bodies and a white tail.

Habitat: Grasslands, open areas, sagebrush flats at low to moderate elevations.

Comments: Usually spotted alone or in pairs in open country during breeding season. In winter, groups of up to 12 may roost together.

SWAINSON'S HAWK
Buteo swainsoni

Size: 18–22 in. (45–55 cm)

Description: Distinguished from other hawks by its tapering wings and dark, subterminal tail band. Black and white pattern on the underwing is also distinctive. The rare dark morph of this species is dark brown below.

Habitat: Open plains, grasslands, prairies.

Comments: A summer resident in Colorado. Most make a 17,000 mi. (27000 km) trip to their wintering grounds in Argentina.

Light Morph

Light Morph

Dark Morph

OWLS

These square-shaped birds of prey have large heads, large eyes and hooked bills. Large flattened areas around each eye form 'facial disks' that help to amplify sound toward external ear flaps. Primarily nocturnal. Genders are similar.

GREAT HORNED OWL
Bubo virginianus

Size: 20–25 in. (50–63 cm)

Description: Large, dark brown bird has heavily barred plumage, ear tufts, yellow eyes and a white throat.

Habitat: Forests, deserts and urban areas.

Comments: Primarily nocturnal, it feeds on small mammals and birds. Occasionally spotted hunting during the day. Call is a deep, resonant – hoo-HOO-hoooo.

BURROWING OWL
Athene cunicularia

Size: 9–11 in. (23–28 cm)

Description: Small terrestrial owl has long legs and yellow eyes.

Habitat: Grassy fields, open plains, dry pastures, airports.

Comments: Usually spotted hunting snakes, mice and lizards on the ground during the day. Inhabits abandoned prairie dog burrows or fox dens. A summer resident statewide.

CHICKEN-LIKE BIRDS

Ground-dwelling birds that are chicken-like in looks and habit. Most have stout bills, rounded wings and heavy bodies. Primarily ground-dwelling, they are capable of short bursts of flight.

WILD TURKEY
Meleagris gallopavo

Size: 34–48 in. (85–120 cm)

Description: Large dark bird has a bluish head, red facial wattles and a rust, fan-shaped tail. Females do not strut or fan their tails.

Habitat: Oak and pine woodlands to 9,000 ft. (2700 m).

Comments: Call is similar to a barnyard turkey. Feeds on acorns, fruit and seeds and roosts in trees at night. In May, the males begin exuberant dances to attract mates.

RING-NECKED PHEASANT
Phasianus colchicus

Size: 30–36 in. (75–90 cm)

Description: Large bird has a long tail, green head and white neck ring. Female is mottled brown with a long tail.

Habitat: Brushy areas, farmland, woodland edges.

Comments: Feeds on seeds, plant shoots and insects. Male defends territory by giving crowing calls and making drumming sounds with its wings.

GAMBEL'S QUAIL
Callipepla gambelii

Size: 9–12 in. (23–30 cm)

Description: Plump bird has a blue neck and upper breast, a buff belly and forward-curving plume (teardrop topknot). Male has black face and belly patches.

Habitat: Deserts.

Comments: One of the more commonly observed desert birds, it typically scurries around the desert floor in small groups called coveys.

GREATER SAGE-GROUSE
Centrocercus urophasianus

Size: 22–30 in. (55–75 cm)

Description: Large bird has a black belly and a pointed tail. Males inflate large breast sacs when dancing during breeding season.

Habitat: Sagebrush shrublands to 8,000 ft. (2400 m).

Comments: The largest of Colorado's grouse species, it can weigh up to 6 lbs. (2.7 kg). In spring, the males gather on dancing grounds called "leks" to attract females.

DUSKY GROUSE
Dendragapus obscurus

Size: 18–22 in. (45–53 cm)

Description: Males are gray or blue-gray and have a colorful red to yellow comb above the eye.

Habitat: Forests from 6,500–11,000 ft. (1950–3300 m).

Comments: During breeding season, males hoot loudly to attract females. Seasonally migrates up and down the mountains. The most abundant and widespread grouse in Colorado.

WHITE-TAILED PTARMIGAN
Lagopus leucurus

Size: 12–14 in. (30–35 cm)

Description: Plumage is mottled brown and white in summer and all-white in winter.

Habitat: Forests, meadows and alpine areas in central Colorado above 11,000 ft. (3300 m).

Comments: Spends most of its life at or near the timberline and feeds on insects, buds, flowers and seeds. Though relatively common in alpine areas, it is often difficult to see due to its coloration that helps it blend in perfectly with its seasonal environments.

GREATER PRAIRIE CHICKEN
Tympanuchus cupido

Size: 16–18 in. (40–45 cm)

Description: Brownish birds are heavily barred. The male inflates its colorful neck sacs during breeding season.

Habitat: Tallgrass prairie, parkland.

Comments: Tours to the breeding areas in Colorado to observe the males performing their spectacular displays are available in March–April.

DOVES & ALLIES

These familiar birds are common and widespread. All species coo. They feed largely on seeds, grain and insects.

ROCK PIGEON
Columba livia

Size: 12–13 in. (30–33 cm)

Description: Blue-gray bird has a white rump and black-banded tail. White, tan and brown variants also occur.

Habitat: Common in urban and rural settings.

Comments: One of the few birds that occur in a variety of colors and patterns, a result of selective breeding of captive birds.

MOURNING DOVE
Zenaida macroura

Size: 11–13 in. (28–33 cm)

Description: Slender tawny bird has a long, pointed tail.

Habitat: Open woodlands, urban areas.

Comments: Named for its mournful cooing song. Often seen perched on powerlines beside roads. The most widespread and abundant dove in the U.S.

HUMMINGBIRDS

The smallest of all birds, hummingbirds are named for the noise made by their wings during flight. All have long, needle-like bills and long tongues that are used to extract nectar from flowers.

BLACK-CHINNED HUMMINGBIRD
Archilochus alexandri

Size: 3–4 in. (8–10 cm)

Description: Small metallic green bird has a black chin and a purplish neck band. Females lack chin and neck markings.

Habitat: Urban areas, wooded canyons to middle elevations.

Comments: One of seven Colorado hummingbirds, it and the broad-tailed hummingbird are the only two to breed regularly in the state.

BROAD-TAILED HUMMINGBIRD
Selasphorus platycercus

Size: 4–5 in. (10–13 cm)

Description: Small, iridescent green bird has a rose red throat and a broad tail. Note white line under its bill.

Habitat: Meadows, grasslands from the plains to the timberline.

Comments: Wings produce a cricket-like trilling sound in flight.

KINGFISHERS

Solitary, broad-billed birds renowned for their fishing skill.

BELTED KINGFISHER
Megaceryle alcyon

Size: 10–15 in. (25–38 cm)

Description: Stocky, crested blue-gray bird with a large head and a stout bill. Female has a rust chest band.

Habitat: Near ponds, lakes and rivers throughout Colorado.

Comments: Often seen perched over clear water. Hovers over water before plunging headfirst after fish. Call is a loud, dry rattle. Feeds on small fish, crayfish, insects, small rodents, salamanders and berries. Most abundant in Colorado in the winter when northern migrants move south for the winter.

♂

♀

WOODPECKERS

These strong-billed birds are usually spotted on tree trunks chipping away bark in search of insects. All have stiff tails that serve as props as they forage. In spring, males drum on dead limbs and other resonant objects (e.g., garbage cans, drainpipes) to establish their territories.

NORTHERN FLICKER
Colaptes auratus

Size: 10–14 in. (25–35 cm)

Description: Brownish woodpecker has a spotted breast and black bib. Yellow-shafted morphs have a red nape patch and yellow wing linings; males have a black mustache. Red-shafted morphs have reddish wing linings; males have a red mustache.

Habitat: Rural and urban woodlands, deserts.

Comments: Feeds on insects. Unlike other woodpeckers it is often seen foraging on the ground. White rump patch flashes during flight. The yellow-shafted morph is the most common Colorado woodpecker.

Yellow-shafted   Red-shafted

DOWNY WOODPECKER
Picoides pubescens

Size: 5–7 in. (13–18 cm)

HAIRY WOODPECKER
Picoides villosus

Size: 8–10 in. (20–25 cm)

Description: Black-and-white woodpeckers have a red head patch. The downy woodpecker is smaller and has a shorter bill.

Habitat: Wooded areas statewide.

Comments: Often seen in parklands and urban areas, both species are common at backyard feeders in winter.

Downy

Hairy

LEWIS' WOODPECKER
Melanerpes lewis

Size: 9–12 in. (23–30 cm)

Description: Greenish woodpecker is distinguished by its gray collar and pinkish belly.

Habitat: Open woodlands, grasslands.

Comments: Feeds primarily on flying insects. It caches acorns and other nuts for winter.

FLYCATCHERS

These compact birds characteristically sit on exposed perches and dart out to catch passing insects.

SAY'S PHOEBE
Sayornis saya
Size: 7–8 in. (18–20 cm)
Description: Gray-brown above, throat is pale gray and underparts are cinnamon.
Habitat: Dry open areas statewide.
Comments: An early spring migrant to Colorado, it arrives as early as March and stays until mid-September.

WESTERN WOOD-PEWEE
Contopus sordidulus
Size: 6–7 in. (15–18 cm)
Description: Greenish to brown above, lighter below. Note two narrow white wing bars.
Habitat: Open forests and riparian areas.
Comments: Call includes clear whistles and a harsh, descending – *peeer*.

WESTERN KINGBIRD
Tyrannus verticalis
Size: To 8 in. (20 cm)
Description: Grayish above, it has a lemon-yellow belly and square-tipped tail edged in white.
Habitat: Open clearings, roadsides and around well-treed ponds and streams.
Comments: Frequently seen around livestock pastures feeding on flying insects.

LARKS

Primarily terrestrial, slender-billed birds are found in fields with low vegetation.

HORNED LARK
Eremophila alpestris
Size: 7–8 in. (18–20 cm)
Description: Brown bird has a yellow face, dark neck and eye marks and black feathery 'horns'.
Habitat: Open grassy areas throughout Colorado.
Comments: Nests and feeds on the ground. Often found in flocks. Often seen in alpine areas during the summer. Populations are in decline.

SWALLOWS

These acrobatic fliers have short bills, long pointed wings and long tails (often forked). Their wide mouths are adapted for scooping up insects on the wing.

VIOLET-GREEN SWALLOW
Tachycineta thalassina
Size: 4–6 in. (10–15 cm)

Description: Plumage is glossy green-purple above, white below. White flank patches nearly meet above the tail.

Habitat: Open and semi-wooded areas in towns, farms and foothills.

Comments: Often seen perched in groups along power lines and fences. Flight is undulating and graceful.

TREE SWALLOW
Tachycineta bicolor
Size: 5–6 in. (13–15 cm)

Description: Plumage is glossy blue-green above and white below. Females are brownish above and white below.

Habitat: Wooded areas near water.

Comments: Despite its name, it inhabits open areas including fields, meadows and marshes and only uses trees for nesting.

BARN SWALLOW
Hirundo rustica
Size: 6–8 in. (15–20 cm)

Description: Blue-black above, cinnamon below, it is easily identified in flight by its long, forked tail.

Habitat: Open woods, fields, farms and lakes.

Comments: Commonly nests in building eaves and under bridges.

CLIFF SWALLOW
Petrochelidon pyrrhonota
Size: 5–6 in. (13–15 cm)

Description: Distinguished by its white forehead, square-edged tail and buffy rump patch.

Habitat: Nests in cliffs, river embankments and under bridges and overhanging structures throughout the state.

Comments: Nests in huge colonies that may number in the thousands. Found in Colorado June–September.

CROWS & ALLIES

These large, omnivorous birds are very common. Most have stout bills with bristles near the base. Sexes are similar.

WOODHOUSE'S SCRUB JAY
Aphelocoma woodhouseii
Size: To 13 in. (33 cm)
Description: A streamlined blue bird with a long bill and tail. Key field marks are white throat, incomplete blue necklace and brown back.
Habitat: Juniper and pinyon pine woodlands, foothills.
Comments: Flight is undulating and short, followed by a sweeping glide. Forages on the ground and in trees.

CANADA JAY
Perisoreus canadensis capitalis
Size: 11–14 in. (28–35 cm)
Description: Medium-sized gray birds have rounded heads and long tails. Note partial hood of black-gray.
Habitat: Mixed evergreen forests.
Comments: Often occurs in small groups. Highly gregarious and unafraid of humans, it is common at picnics and campsites begging for food.

PINYON JAY
Gymnorhinus cyanocephalus
Size: 9–12 in. (23–30 cm)
Description: Gray blue bird has a thin, sharp beak and a short tail.
Habitat: Pinyon-juniper forests.
Comments: Feeds primarily on pinyon nuts. Often gathers in large, noisy flocks.

STELLER'S JAY
Cyanocitta stelleri
Size: 12–14 in. (30–35 cm)
Description: Distinguished at a glance by its prominent head crest and deep blue on wings, belly and tail.
Habitat: Pine and pine-oak forests.
Comments: Very gregarious, it frequents campsites and human dwellings in search of handouts.

BLUE JAY
Cyanocitta cristata

Size: To 14 in. (35 cm)

Description: Easily recognized by its crested head, blue back and black neckband.

Habitat: Woodlands and open areas.

Comments: This bold, aggressive bird often dominates backyard feeders. It has several vocalizations, some of which are quite musical. Call is a loud – *jay-jay-jay*!

BLACK-BILLED MAGPIE
Pica hudsonia

Size: To 22 in. (55 cm)

Description: Beautifully marked black-and-white bird with a long tail. Iridescent plumage shines green, blue, purple and bronze.

Habitat: Forests, foothills and cities throughout Colorado to elevations of 10,000 ft. (3000 m).

Comments: Flashy, loud and boisterous birds are easily spotted in a variety of habitats. Feeds on berries, fruit, small animals and carrion.

COMMON RAVEN
Corvus corax

Size: 21–27 in. (53–68 cm)

Description: A large black bird with a heavy bill, wedge-shaped tail and shaggy head and throat feathers.

Habitat: Mountains, canyons in central to western Colorado.

Comments: Distinguished from crows by its large size and low, croaking call. Despite its call, it is classified as a songbird. Feeds primarily on insects, small animals and carrion.

AMERICAN CROW
Corvus brachyrhynchos

Size: 18–21 in. (45–53 cm)

Description: Black bird has a thick black bill. Call is a distinct – *caw*.

Habitat: Fields, beaches, forests, parks, cities.

Comments: Abundant and widespread, they do a valuable service in controlling insect populations.

DIPPERS

Plump, energetic, stubby-tailed birds feed along waterways.

AMERICAN DIPPER
Cinclus mexicanus
Size: To 7 in. (18 cm)

Description: Chunky, soot-gray bird has a short tail.

Habitat: Clear, fast-moving streams from the foothills to the timberline.

Comments: Uses its short wings to "fly" underwater where it then walks on the stream bottoms – into the current – and feeds on aquatic insects. Often seen on the streamside rocks where it dips and bobs constantly. Song is a cascade of musical whistled notes.

KINGLETS & BUSHTITS

Tiny active woodland birds are the smallest North American songbirds.

RUBY-CROWNED KINGLET
Regulus calendula
Size: To 4 in. (10 cm)

Description: Tiny plump bird has olive-gray plumage and white wing bars. The scarlet crown patch is most evident when the male is excited.

Habitat: Coniferous and mixed woodlands.

Comments: Is very active and often flicks its wings when perching, which helps to distinguish it from similar warblers. The golden-crowned kinglet (*R. satrapa*) is also found in Colorado.

Golden-crowned Kinglet

BUSHTIT
Psaltriparus minimus
Size: To 4 in. (10 cm)

Description: Tiny, brown to gray bird with a relatively large, rounded head and short bill. Note gray crown and brown ear patch.

Habitat: Open woodlands and scrubby areas, suburbs and parks to 11,000 ft. (3300 m).

Comments: Call is a sharp twittering. Eats mostly small insects and spiders and feeds in large flocks. Builds a hanging nest using spider webs and plant material.

WRENS

This family of birds has the distinctive habit of cocking their tails in the air when perching.

HOUSE WREN
Troglodytes aedon

Size: 4–5 in. (10–13 cm)

Description: Distinguished by its barred, cocked tail and slender bill.

Habitat: Thickets, wooded areas, farmlands, towns.

Comments: An aggressive little bird, it moves about in quick, jerky motions, often scolding intruders. Common at birdbaths and feeders. The canyon wren (*Catherpes mexicanus*) is common in canyons and cliffs throughout Colorado and is more often seen than heard. Its sharp, clear call of a descending, decelerating series of 7–12 *tee* and *tew* notes is a common wilderness sound.

Canyon Wren

NUTHATCHES

Nuthatches are stout little birds with thin, sharp bills and stumpy tails.

WHITE-BREASTED NUTHATCH
Sitta carolinensis

Size: 5–6 in. (13–15 cm)

Description: Chunky, white-faced, grayish bird has a black cap, white underparts and a short, sharp bill.

Habitat: Coniferous forests, mixed woodlands and riparian areas.

Comments: Creeps about on tree trunks and branches searching for insects, often descending head first. Call is a distinct nasal – *yank, yank*.

RED-BREASTED NUTHATCH
Sitta canadensis

Size: To 4.5 in. (11 cm)

Description: Chunky, white-faced, grayish bird with black cap and eye line, rusty underparts and a short, sharp bill.

Habitat: Coniferous forests.

Comments: Call sounds like a tiny tin horn – *enk, enk*. Easily attracted to feeders with suet in winter.

CREEPERS

Small, stiff-tailed birds have slightly downcurved, thin bills.

BROWN CREEPER
Certhia americana

Size: 5–6 in. (13–15 cm)

Description: Small, slim brown bird is brown above, light below with a thin, decurved bill and a stiff, woodpecker-like tail.

Habitat: Found in deciduous and mixed forests and woodlands.

Comments: Uses stiff tail as a stabilizer while it forages for insects up and down tree trunks and branches. Song is appropriately a thin – *trees, trees, trees.*

CHICKADEES & ALLIES

These small, friendly birds with short bills and long tails often occur in small flocks.

MOUNTAIN CHICKADEE
Poecile gambeli

Size: To 5 in. (13 cm)

Description: Small grayish bird has a black crown, chin and eye stripe.

Habitat: Coniferous forests, mixed woodlands, towns.

Comments: Gregarious bird is most common in forests and mountainous areas. Call is a hoarse – *chick-adee-dee-dee.*

BLACK-CAPPED CHICKADEE
Poecile atricapillus

Size: To 6 in. (15 cm)

Description: Distinguished by its fluffy plumage and black cap and bib. The boreal chickadee has a brown cap and a black bib.

Habitat: Forests, open woodlands, suburbs.

Comments: Call is a 2–3 note, whistled – *fee-bee –* or a clear – c*hick-a-dee-dee-dee-dee.* Common at feeders in winter.

JUNIPER TITMOUSE
Baeolophus ridgwayi
Size: To 6 in. (15 cm)
Description: Small, fluffy gray bird has a prominent head crest.
Habitat: Pinyon-juniper woodlands in western and southern Colorado.
Comments: Song is a rapid and rolling series of 5–15 syllables with a uniform pitch.

THRUSHES
This group of woodland birds includes many good singers. Sexes are similar in most.

MOUNTAIN BLUEBIRD
Sialia currucoides
Size: 6–8 in. (15–20 cm)
Description: Long-tailed sky-blue bird is unmistakable.
Habitat: Mountainous areas and forest edges to 14,000 ft. (4200 m).
Comments: Primarily a summer resident, a few overwinter in southern Colorado.

WESTERN BLUEBIRD
Sialia mexicana
Size: 6–7 in. (15–18 cm)
Description: Male is bright blue above with a rust breast and white belly. Female is brownish with dull blue wings and tail.
Habitat: Open woodlands and grasslands at mid to upper elevations.
Comments: Often seen on exposed perches when hunting for insects.

AMERICAN ROBIN
Turdus migratorius
Size: 9–11 in. (23–28 cm)
Description: Gray bird has a rust breast.
Habitat: Ranges from oak woodlands to coniferous forests.
Comments: Forages on the ground for insects, snails and worms. Most common in high country.

TOWNSEND'S SOLITAIRE
Myadestes townsendi
Size: 8–10 in. (20–25 cm)

Description: Slim gray bird has a white eye ring, buffy side patches and a white-edged tail.

Habitat: Coniferous forests to the treeline, open and scrubby juniper woodlands in winter.

Comments: Renowned for its rich, loud, melodious warbling song. Feeds on juniper berries in winter.

WAXWINGS

These gregarious birds are named for their red wing marks that look like waxy droplets.

CEDAR WAXWING
Bombycilla cedrorum
Size: 6–8 in. (15–20 cm)

Description: Told by its sleek, crested head, yellow belly, yellow-tipped tail and red wing marks.

Habitat: Open deciduous woods, orchards, urban areas.

Comments: Diet consists largely of berries and insects. Typically occurs in small flocks.

SHRIKES

Shrikes are carnivorous birds that feed on insects, small birds and rodents.

LOGGERHEAD SHRIKE
Lanius ludovicianus
Size: 8–10 in. (20–25 cm)

Description: Gray-backed bird has a black mask and a stout, hooked bill.

Habitat: Forests and open areas including deserts and grasslands.

Comments: Flight is undulating. Often seen perching atop trees and telephone wires in open country. Infamously known as "butcher birds" they will store their prey in the forks of tree branches or skewered on thorns or barbed wire.

STARLINGS

These fat-bodied, short-tailed birds are abundant in cities and towns. An introduced species.

EUROPEAN STARLING
Sturnus vulgaris
Size: 6–8 in. (15–20 cm)
Description: Chubby bird has iridescent black-purple plumage and a pointed yellow bill.
Habitat: Farms, fields, urban and riparian areas statewide.
Comments: Considered a pest by many, the starling is an aggressive bird that outcompetes native species for food and nesting sites. First arrived in Colorado in 1937 and has since become widespread throughout the state in most habitats. Often occurs in huge flocks (murmurations) in fall and winter.

WARBLERS & ALLIES

Members of this large family of highly active, insect-eating birds are distinguished from other small birds by their thin, pointed bills. Males tend to be more brightly colored than females and are the only singers. Those that are migrants tend to be duller-colored than shown here.

YELLOW-RUMPED WARBLER
Setophaga coronata
Size: 5–6 in. (13–15 cm)
Description: Blue gray above, it has a yellow cap, rump and wing patches. Two races exist. The Myrtle race has a white throat; the Audubon's race has a yellow throat.
Habitat: Coniferous and mixed forests.
Comments: Vivid and conspicuous when foraging, it sings from tree canopies.

Myrtle Race

Audubon Race

YELLOW WARBLER
Setophaga petechia
Size: 4–5.5 in. (10–14 cm)
Description: Distinctive yellow bird has a reddish streaked breast.
Habitat: Wooded and urban areas to 9,500 ft. (2850 m).
Comments: The most conspicuous and widespread Colorado warbler. Song is a cheery ▪ *sweet, sweet, sweet*

BLACKBIRDS & ALLIES

A diverse group of birds ranging from iridescent black birds to brightly-colored meadowlarks and orioles. All have conical, sharply-pointed bills.

WESTERN MEADOWLARK
Sturnella neglecta

Size: 8–11 in. (20–28 cm)

Description: Mottled brown bird is distinguished by its bright yellow breast, white-edged tail and dark V-shaped neckband.

Habitat: Grassy fields, meadows, plains statewide.

Comments: Loud, flute-like, gurgling song is distinctive.

RED-WINGED BLACKBIRD
Agelaius phoeniceus

Size: 8–10 in. (20–25 cm)

Description: Male is black with prominent red shoulder patches. Females are brownish.

Habitat: Sloughs, marshes and wet fields to 9,000 ft. (2700 m).

Comments: Usually nests in reeds or tall grass near water. Gurgling song – *konk-la-REE* – is a common wetland sound. An early spring migrant, it often arrives before the winter snows have melted.

BREWER'S BLACKBIRD
Euphagus cyanocephalus

Size: 8–10 in. (20–25 cm)

Description: Black plumage has a purplish sheen. Female is gray-brown. Eyes are yellow or white.

Habitat: Grasslands, fields, parks.

Comments: Roosts in large colonies at night.

GREAT-TAILED GRACKLE
Quiscalus mexicanus

Size: 16–17 in. (40–43 cm)

Description: Purplish-black bird has a long tail shaped like a boat's keel. Eyes are yellow. Females are brown above with buffy underparts.

Habitat: Towns, fields.

Comments: Call includes a series of whistles and harsh creaks.

COMMON GRACKLE
Quiscalus quiscula
Size: To 14 in. (35 cm)
Description: Black-purple bird has a long, wedge-shaped tail and yellow eyes.
Habitat: Open woods, fields, parks, lawns.
Comments: Common in Colorado during breeding season in spring–summer.

BROWN-HEADED COWBIRD
Molothrus ater
Size: 6–8 in. (15–20 cm)
Description: Metallic green-black bird has a brown hood and a heavy bill.
Habitat: Open woods, farmlands and fields, often near domestic livestock.
Comments: Female is noted for her parasitic habit of laying eggs in the nests of other birds. While some species remove the new egg, most will raise the cowbird as their own, often at the expense of their young.

BULLOCK'S ORIOLE
Icterus bullockii
Size: To 9 in. (23 cm)
Description: Distinctive black and orange bird has a black cap, chin and eyestripe and a white wing patch.
Habitat: Open deciduous forests, ranchlands.
Comments: Like most orioles, it weaves distinctive pouch-shaped nests out of grasses and twigs.

YELLOW-HEADED BLACKBIRD
Xanthocephalus xanthocephalus
Size: To 11 in. (28 cm)
Description: Red-winged male is black with prominent red shoulder patches. Yellow-headed male is unmistakable.
Habitat: Sloughs, marshes and wet fields.
Comments: Usually nests in reeds or tall grass near water. Normally found in large flocks.

TANAGERS

These brightly-colored birds of tropical origin have heavy, conical, seed-cracking bills.

WESTERN TANAGER
Piranga ludoviciana

Size: 6–7 in. (15–18 cm)

Description: Yellow bird has a red head and a dark back. Females and young are olive-colored with 2 light wing bars.

Habitat: Open coniferous and mixed forests.

Comments: Gregarious bird is common near picnic areas. Call is a slurred – *pit-ick, pit-ick.*

FINCHES, SPARROWS & ALLIES

Members of this family have short, thick, seed-cracking bills.

SPOTTED TOWHEE
Pipilo maculatus

Size: To 8 in. (20 cm)

Description: Told by black hood, rufous sides, white belly and red eyes. Female is brown where male is black.

Habitat: Woodlands, wood margins, cities, usually in undergrowth.

Comments: Typically feeds in the undergrowth on seeds and insects.

AMERICAN GOLDFINCH
Spinus tristis

Size: 4–6 in. (10–15 cm)

Description: Male is bright yellow with a black cap, black tail and wings and a white rump. Duller female lacks a cap.

Habitat: Wooded groves, gardens.

Comments: Often found in flocks. Can be identified on the wing by its deeply undulating flight. Canary-like song is bright and cheery. The lesser goldfinch (*S. psaltria*) is also found in Colorado in small flocks in the foothills and fields Male has a black cap, a black or greenish back, yellow underparts and bold white wing marks. Duller female lacks a cap.

Lesser
Goldfinch

HOUSE FINCH
Haemorhous mexicanus
Size: 5–6 in. (13–15 cm)
Description: Brown bird has a reddish forehead, streaked breast and rump.
Habitat: Deserts to oak woodlands, urban areas.
Comments: A highly social bird, it is easily attracted to feeders and nesting sites. Known for its cheerful, twittering song.

♀

♂

DARK-EYED JUNCO
Junco hyemalis
Size: 5–7 in. (13–18 cm)
Description: Key field marks are dark head, whitish bill, white belly and white-edged tail.
Has gray sides and a gray back or a black head and a brown back.
Habitat: Coniferous and mixed woods, gardens, parks.
Comments: Gregarious and easily attracted to feeders. A relatively newly designated species, formerly the slate-colored junco, Oregon junco, gray-headed junco and white-winged junco.

Pink-sided Race

Oregon Race

Slate-colored Race

Gray-headed Race

CHIPPING SPARROW
Spizella passerina

Size: 5–6 in. (13–15 cm)

Description: Told by red cap, white eyebrow line, unstreaked breast and notched tail.

Habitat: Open forests, fields, lawns, gardens.

Comments: Nests are often victimized by brown-headed cowbirds that lay their eggs for the sparrows to raise. Song is a repetitive, sharp – *chip*.

SONG SPARROW
Melospiza melodia

Size: 5–7 in. (13–18 cm)

Description: Distinguished by heavily-streaked breast with streaks converging to a central spot. Tail is rounded.

Habitat: Very common in bushes and woodlands near water.

Comments: Often visits feeders and birdbaths. Forages along the ground. Melodious song usually begins with 3–4 similar notes.

EVENING GROSBEAK
Coccothraustes vespertinus

Size: To 8 in. (20 cm)

Description: A stocky yellow and black bird with prominent white wing-patch.

Habitat: Found in deciduous forests, a frequent visitor to urban areas in winter.

Comments: In winter, it feeds on fruiting shrubs and feeders.

LARK BUNTING
Calamospiza melanocorys

Size: 6–7 in. (15–18 cm)

Description: Black prairie bird has a prominent white wing patch.

Habitat: Shortgrass prairie in eastern Colorado to the foothills.

Comments: A migrant bird, flocks arrive in April and inhabit the region until September. Found at elevations up to 8,000 ft. (2400 m).

Colorado's State Bird

RED CROSSBILL
Loxia curvirostra
Size: 6–7 in. (15–18 cm)
Description: Chunky brick-red bird has a large head, plain wings and a thick bill that is crossed at the tip. Females are olive to yellowish.
Habitat: Coniferous forests.
Comments: Its presence is often detected by the loud cracking sound it makes when dissecting conifer cones.

WHITE-CROWNED SPARROW
Zonotrichia leucophrys
Size: To 8 in. (20 cm)
Description: White crown is bordered by black stripes.
Habitat: Nests in dense brush near grasslands.
Comments: Feeds most often on the ground.

PINE SISKIN
Spinus pinus
Size: 4–5 in. (10–13 cm)
Description: Brown bird has heavily streaked plumage and a notched tail. Small yellow patches on wings and tail are most prominent in flight.
Habitat: Coniferous and mixed forests.
Comments: Quite tame and easily attracted to feeders. Often found flocking in the tops of trees.

WEAVER FINCHES

These sparrow-like birds were introduced to North America in 1850, and are now widespread throughout the continent.

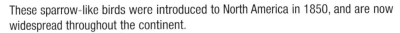

HOUSE SPARROW
Passer domesticus
Size: 5–6 in. (13–15 cm)
Description: Black throat and brown nape of male are key field marks. Females and young are dull brown with a light eye stripe.
Habitat: Suburbs, cities, farmlands.
Comments: These gregarious, social birds gather in large flocks between breeding seasons.

The diverse habitats of Colorado make it a prime location to find and study reptiles and amphibians. In total, there are over 70 species.

REPTILES

Reptiles can generally be described as terrestrial, scaly-skinned creatures that breathe through lungs. The majority reproduce by laying eggs on land. In some, the eggs develop inside the mother who later gives birth to live young. Contrary to popular belief, very few are harmful to man and many are valuable in controlling rodent and insect populations. The most common types of reptiles in Colorado are:

Turtles

Lizards

Snakes

AMPHIBIANS

Amphibians are smooth-skinned, limbed vertebrates that live in moist habitats and breathe through lungs, skin, gills or a combination of all three. While many spend much of their lives on land, they still depend on a watery environment to complete their life cycle. Most reproduce by laying eggs in or near water. The young hatch as swimming larvae that breathe through gills. After a short developmental period, the larvae metamorphose into young adults with lungs and legs. The most common types of Colorado amphibians are:

Salamanders

Frogs

Toads

How to Find Reptiles & Amphibians

Reptiles are secretive but can be observed if you know where to look. Turtles are found on the edges of ponds and lakes and often sun themselves on rocks and logs. Lizards sun themselves in habitats ranging from open deserts to suburban back yards and are the most conspicuous reptiles. Snakes can be found in deserts, canyons and along trails and watercourses. When seeking reptiles, be careful. Many snakes are well-camouflaged and can be sluggish in the morning or after eating. Do not put hands in places you can't see into. Turn over rocks and logs with a stick or tool. Frogs are found in wet areas on or near the water. Toads are more terrestrial and may be found far from water, especially during the day. Salamanders are more secretive and rarely venture out of their cool, moist habitats.

TURTLES

Turtles are easily distinguished by their large bony carapaces (shells), which serve to protect them from most predators. Like all reptiles, turtles breathe air through lungs; they are also able to breathe underwater from gill-like respiratory surfaces on the mouth and anus. Turtles are most active in spring during mating season. Most are omnivores and eat a wide variety of plant and animal matter.

WESTERN PAINTED TURTLE
Chrysemys picta bellii

Size: 4–10 in. (10–25 cm)
Description: Greenish aquatic turtle has narrow yellow streaks on its head. Plastron (lower shell) is red.
Habitat: Ponds, marshes, lakes, ditches, streams.
Comments: Typically lives in well-vegetated shallow waters. Feeds on vegetation, insects, mollusks, crayfish and other invertebrates.

Colorado's State Reptile

SNAPPING TURTLE
Chelydra serpentina

Size: To 18 in. (45 cm)
Description: Distinguished by its rough, knobby shell and long tail that is saw-toothed on its upper edge.
Habitat: Ponds and lakes with muddy bottoms in eastern Colorado.
Comments: An aggressive predator, it feeds on fishes, amphibians, reptiles, mammals and birds. It should be treated with caution when encountered on land as it will often lunge at humans and can inflict serious cuts.

ORNATE BOX TURTLE
Terrapene ornata ornata

Size: 4–6 in. (10–15 cm)
Description: Domed shell has radiating light lines and is flattened on the top. Lines are often broken into spots. Sturdy limbs and long claws are well-adapted for digging.
Habitat: Prairie grasslands and open woodlands with sandy soil in eastern Colorado to 5,500 ft. (1750 m).
Comments: Found primarily on land, it feeds on insects and invertebrates, carrion, berries, cactus fruits and pads. A protected species in Colorado.

Shell closed

Hinged plastron (lower shell) allows it to retract its head, neck and limbs completely into its shell when threatened.

LIZARDS

Lizards are scaly-skinned animals that usually have 4 legs and a tail, movable eyelids, visible ear openings, claws and toothed jaws. A few species are legless and superficially resemble snakes. Lizards represent the largest group of living reptiles and range in size from tiny skinks to the giant 10-foot-long monitor lizards of Indonesia. Ten species are found in Colorado.

COLLARED LIZARD
Crotaphytus collaris

Size: 9–14 in. (23–35 cm)

Description: Conspicuous, greenish, long-tailed lizard has two dark collar markings.

Habitat: Rocky areas in deserts, foothills and forests to 6,000 ft. (1800 m).

Comments: It flees danger by running swiftly on its hind legs. Will bite readily if handled. Spends winters in an underground den.

GREATER SHORT-HORNED LIZARD
Phrynosoma hernandesi

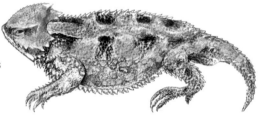

Size: 4–6 in. (10–15 cm)

Description: Brown to gray lizard is covered with short, stubby horns and has one row of fringe scales.

Habitat: Prairies, deserts, forests with sandy or rocky soil.

Comments: Feeds during the day on insects, especially ants. When threatened, it is capable of squirting blood from its eyes at predators. Often misnamed "horned toads".

FENCE LIZARD
Sceloporus undulatus

Size: To 8 in. (20 cm)

Description: Mottled brown to grayish, it has keeled scales on its back. Male often has bright blue patches on its throat and along the sides of its belly.

Habitat: Deciduous and coniferous woods, sandy areas, urban gardens.

Comments: Active during the day, it spends much of its time hunting prey in trees and on man-made structures.

GREAT PLAINS SKINK
Plestiodon obsoletus

Size: 6–14 in. (15–35 cm)

Description: Large, elongate, tan to gray lizard has dark-edged scales. Juveniles are black and have a blue tail.

Habitat: Rocky grasslands and dry areas near water.

Comments: The largest North American skink is found in western and central Colorado. Active during the day, it can be found at elevations up to 7,200 ft. (2160 m).

SIX-LINED RACERUNNER
Aspidoscelis sexlineatus

Size: 6–10 in. (15–25 cm)

Description: Brown to black lizard has 6–7 light stripes on its back and sides.

Habitat: Grasslands, dry, sunny areas with well-drained soils in western Colorado.

Comments: Often the most conspicuous lizard in dry habitats, it is very active in the morning.

SNAKES

Snakes are limbless reptiles with dry, scaly skin, toothed jaws, no ear openings or eyelids and a single row of belly scales. They move by contracting their muscles in waves and undulating over the ground. All are carnivorous and swallow their prey whole. The vast majority are harmless to humans.

BULLSNAKE
Pituophis catenifer

Size: To 8 ft. (2.4 m)

Description: Brownish, cream or yellowish snake is covered in dark red, brown or black blotches. Scales are keeled.

Habitat: Dry woodlands, fields, open brushland to 8,500 ft. (2550 m).

Comments: A constrictor, it feeds primarily on rodents it swallows head first. Defensive behavior mimics a rattlesnake's although it lacks a tail rattle. Also called gopher snake.

CENTRAL PLAINS MILK SNAKE
Lampropeltis triangulum gentiles

Size: 18–24 in. (45–60 cm)

Description: Ringed snake is unmistakable.

Habitat: Prairies, woodlands and mountainous areas in eastern Colorado.

Comments: Constrictor is common where rodents are found.

PLAINS GARTER SNAKE
Thamnophis radix
Size: 20–40 in. (50–100 cm)

Description: Easily distinguished by its orange or yellow dorsal stripe. Has row of dark spots between back and pale side stripes.

Habitat: Wet areas, meadows, bogs, prairies, along waterways and lakes.

Comments: Common in urban areas, it feeds on amphibians and small rodents.

YELLOW-BELLIED RACER
Coluber constrictor
Size: 30–60 in. (75–150 cm)

Description: Slender gray, olive or brown snake has smooth scales.

Habitat: Fields, grasslands, meadows, urban gardens to 6,000 ft. (1800 m).

Comments: A fast, agile snake, it is often seen streaking through lawns and crossing roads. Holds head high when hunting. Will bite readily if handled.

GREAT PLAINS RAT SNAKE
Pantherophis emoryi
Size: 3–5 ft. (90–150 cm)

Description: Tan, gray or brownish snake has gray blotching on its back. Stripes on either side of the head form a spear-point mark between the eyes.

Habitat: Rocky hillsides, open grasslands, woodlands, farmlands.

Comments: Primarily nocturnal, it is often spotted near human dwellings hunting mice, rats, birds and bats.

PLAINS HOGNOSE SNAKE
Heterodon nasicus
Size: 15–35 in. (38–88 cm)

Description: Stout-bodied snake has a sharply upturned and pointed snout. Tan, brown or grayish, it is covered in dark blotches down its back.

Habitat: Sandy-soiled grasslands, river floodplains to 6,000 ft. (1800 m) in eastern Colorado.

Comments: Uses upturned snout to dig out toads and prey from loose soil. When threatened, it will mimic a cobra and rise up and flatten its neck and even feign striking. If this fails, it will play dead and excrete a foul-smelling musk.

WESTERN RATTLESNAKE
Crotalus viridis

Size: To 5 ft. (150 cm)

Description: A darkly-blotched, greenish-brown snake with a spade-shaped head, defined neck and tail rattle.

Habitat: Grasslands, brushy areas and woodlands to 11,000 ft. (3350 m).

Comments: A pit viper, it has heat sensing areas between its eyes and nostrils that help it detect prey. Enlarged front fangs have hollow canals that inject poison into prey when it strikes. Eats mostly rodents. Bites are capable of killing humans. The smaller and rarer massauga (*Sistrurus catenatus*) and midget faded rattlesnake (*Crotalus oreganus concolor*) are also found in Colorado. These grow to around 30 in. (75 cm).

Midget-faded
Rattlesnake

Massasauga

SALAMANDERS

Salamanders are smooth-skinned, tailed creatures that lack claws and ear openings. Some have the ability to regenerate tails or limbs lost to predators. Seldom seen, they live in dark, moist habitats and are nocturnal and secretive. They are most active in the spring and fall, especially near the pools where they breed.

Fertilization in most is internal but is not accomplished by copulation. During mating, the male releases a small packet of sperm which the female brushes against and draws into her body. The packet is kept in her body until she ovulates, which may be months later. Most species lay their eggs in water. Both adults and larvae are carnivorous and feed on worms and insects and other invertebrates.

BARRED TIGER SALAMANDER
Ambystoma tigrinum mavortium

Size: 6–12 in. (15–30 cm)

Description: Dark brown to blackish, it has yellowish blotches and spots on its body.

Habitat: Moist habitats in meadows, forests and grasslands at elevations to 12,000 ft. (3600 m).

Comments: Colorado's state amphibian, it is the only amphibian documented in all 64 counties of Colorado. Active primarily at night, it feeds on snails, insects and other invertebrates.

Colorado's State Amphibian

FROGS & TOADS

Frogs and toads are squat amphibians common near ponds and lakes. All have large heads, large eyes, long hind legs and long, sticky tongues that they use to catch insects. Most have well-developed ears and strong voices. Only males are vocal.

Frogs have smooth skin, slim waists and many have prominent dorsal ridges. In most, the male initiates mating by calling for females. When he finds a mate, he clasps her in water and fertilizes the eggs as they are laid. The eggs initially hatch into fish-like tadpoles that breathe through gills and feed on vegetation. They later transform into young adults with limbs and lungs.

Toads can be distinguished from frogs by their dry, warty skin and prominent glands behind their eyes (parotoids). Some also have swellings between their eyes (bosses). When handled roughly by would-be predators, the warts and glands secrete a poisonous substance that makes the toads extremely unpalatable. Contrary to popular belief, handling toads does not cause warts.

CHORUS FROG
Pseudacris triseriata
Size: 1–2 in. (3–5 cm)
Description: Green-gray to brown frog has three dark stripes down its back and a dark stripe through the eye.
Habitat: Ponds, marshes, reservoirs, wet meadows.
Comments: Call is a rasping trill that sounds like running a fingernail over the teeth of a comb.

NORTHERN LEOPARD FROG
Lithobates pipiens
Size: To 5 in. (13 cm)
Description: Slender green or brown frog is covered in light-edged dark spots. Has light-colored dorsolateral ridges down its back.
Habitat: Well-vegetated ponds and streams, marshes and wet fields.
Comments: Call is a low, rattling snore followed by clucking notes. Primarily nocturnal, it is more often heard than seen.

Tadpole

BULLFROG
Lithobates catesbeianus
Size: 4–8 in. (10–20 cm)
Description: Large green to yellowish frog has a rounded snout. Eardrum is as large as the eye.
Habitat: Ponds, lakes, slow-moving waterways.
Comments: Call is a deep-pitched – *jurrrooom.* A voracious predator, it will eat anything it can swallow. The largest North American frog has been introduced to Colorado from the eastern U.S.

Tadpole

WESTERN TOAD
Anaxyrus boreas
Size: 3–5 in. (8–15 cm)
Description: Gray to green toad has a cream-colored dorsal stripe.
Habitat: Near water in meadows and woodlands in western Colorado.
Comments: Active at dawn and dusk. Males have a soft, clucking call like the peeping of chicks.

WOODHOUSES'S TOAD
Anaxyrus woodhousii
Size: 3–5 in. (8–13 cm)
Description: Yellowish to gray, it has prominent head crests and a light stripe down the middle of its back. Has prominent head crests and elongate glands (*parotids*) behind the eyes.
Habitat: Sandy areas, marshes, urban green spaces to 7,000 ft. (2100 m).
Comments: Primarily nocturnal, it is often seen foraging for prey near outdoor lights. Call is a nasal, sheep-like bleating.

PLAINS SPADEFOOT TOAD
Scaphiopus bombifrons
Size: To 2.5 in. (6 cm)
Description: Brown, green or gray toad is covered in dark blotches. Has a bony lump between its eyes. Note vertical pupils.
Habitat: Prairies and areas with sandy and gravelly soils in eastern and central Colorado.
Comments: Nocturnal. Named for the wedge-shaped spade on each hind foot that it uses for digging its daytime burrow.

Fishes are cold-blooded vertebrates that live in water and breathe dissolved oxygen through organs called gills. They are generally characterized by their size, shape, feeding habits and water temperature preference. Most live in either saltwater or freshwater, though a few species divide their lives between the two (these are referred to as anadromous fishes).

Most fishes have streamlined bodies and swim by flexing their bodies from side to side. Their fins help to steer while swimming and can also act as brakes. Many species possess an internal air bladder that acts as a depth regulator. By secreting gases into the bladder or absorbing gases from it, they are able to control the depth at which they swim.

Most fish reproduce by laying eggs freely in the water. In many, the male discharges sperm over the eggs as they are laid by the female. Depending on the species, eggs may float, sink, become attached to vegetation or be buried.

How to Identify Fishes

First, note the size, shape and color of the fish. Are there any distinguishing field marks like the double dorsal fins of the basses or the downturned lips of the suckers? Is the body thin or torpedo-shaped? Note the orientation and placement of fins on the body. Consult the text to confirm identification. The species in this guide include the most popular game fishes in Colorado.

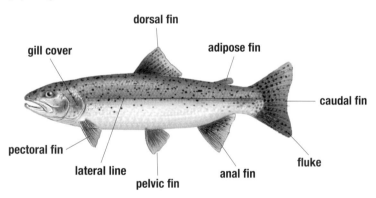

SAFELY RELEASING A FISH

A number of Colorado fishes must be returned unharmed to the water if hooked (see end of section). The steps to follow include:

1. Keep the fish in the water as much as possible and hold gently. Avoid squeezing.
2. Using a pair of forceps or long-nosed pliers, safely remove the hook. If the fish is hooked too deeply, cut the line as close to the hook as possible.
3. To release fish, gently hold it under the water. Point its head into the current and move it slowly backward and forward to deliver more oxygen to its gills. It will start to wriggle away when revived.

RAINBOW TROUT
Oncorhynchus mykiss
Size: To 2 ft. (60 cm)

Description: Dark-spotted fish is named for the distinctive reddish band running down its side. Band is most prominent during spring spawning.

Habitat: Abundant in cold streams, reservoirs and lakes.

Comments: Introduced in the 1880s, it has become the mainstay of Colorado's Hatchery System, which releases millions of fish annually.

CUTTHROAT (NATIVE) TROUT
Oncorhynchus clarkii
Size: To 39 in. (98 cm)

Description: Distinguished from rainbow by its red throat slash and heavier spotting toward the tail.

Habitat: High elevation lakes and streams.

Comments: Three subspecies of trout are native to Colorado. Widespread introduction of non-native salmonids including the rainbow trout have severely limited their range, which is now primarily in isolated headwater streams. The greenback trout was limited to a few remote streams in Rocky Mountain National park and extensive plans have been made to reintroduce the species where viable.

Rio Grande Cutthroat Trout
Oncorhynchus clarkii virginalis – To 39 in. (98 cm)

Greenback Cutthroat Trout
Oncorhynchus clarkii stomias – To 18 in. (45 cm)
Colorado's State Fish

Colorado River Cutthroat Trout
Oncorhynchus clarkii pleuriticus – To 18 in. (45 cm)

LAKE TROUT
Salvelinus namaycush
Size: To 50 in. (1.3 m)

Description: Blue-gray to olive above, its body is covered in pale, irregular spots. Pelvic, pectoral and anal fins are sometimes red-orange with a white leading edge. Caudal fin is deeply forked.

Habitat: Deep, cold lakes and rivers.

Comments: The largest North American trout is a prized food fish. Also called mackinaw, lake char and siscowet.

BROOK TROUT
Salvelinus fontinalis
Size: To 21 in. (53 cm)

Description: Has wavy yellow marks on dorsal side and dorsal fin. Reddish side spots have blue halos. The breeding male is brilliant red-orange below and has a black belly.

Habitat: Clear, freshwater streams and rivers; some are anadromous.

Comments: An introduced sport fish weighing up to 14 lbs. (6.3 kg).

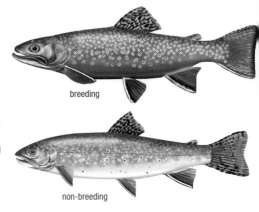
breeding

non-breeding

SPLAKE
Salvelinus fontinalis x Salvelinus namaycush
Size: To 40 in. (1 m)

Description: A hybrid species of lake and brook trout it has tri-colored pelvic fins like brook trout and its tail is slightly forked like the lake trout.

Habitat: Clear freshwater streams and rivers, seeks deeper cooler water during the summer months.

Comments: A prized sport fish in summer, it weighs up to 18 lbs. (8 kg).

BROWN TROUT
Salmo trutta
Size: To 40 in. (1 m)

Description: Olive to brown above, it is covered with red, black or orange spots, often with white halos. Caudal fin is straight-edged. Breeding male has a hooked jaw and is reddish, orangish or yellowish on its sides and belly. It often has red or orange on its adipose fin, a feature unique to this species.

Habitat: Cool streams and lakes.

Comments: An introduced species renowned for its wariness.

breeding

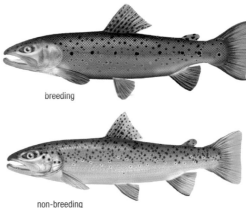
non-breeding

GRAYLING
Thymallus arcticus
Size: To 30 in. (75 cm)

Description: Dark blue-gray above, it is distinguished by its huge, sail-like spotted dorsal fin and forked tail. Mouth is small.

Habitat: Clear, cold rivers and lakes.

Comments: Native to northern drainages, it is a popular sport fish since it can be taken on flies or lures. Spawns in spring in shallow rivers and streams.

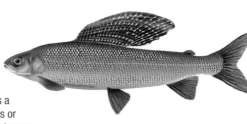

KOKANEE SALMON
Oncorhynchus nerka
Size: To 33 in. (83 cm)

Description: Body is lightly speckled and lacks large black spots on back and caudal fins. Red breeding male has hooked jaws and green head. Tail lacks spotting.

Habitat: Large mountain reservoirs.

Comments: One of the most sought-after Colorado sport fishes.

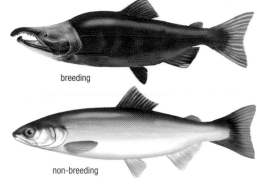

breeding

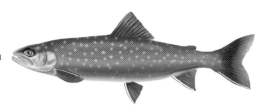

non-breeding

ARCTIC CHAR
Salvelinus alpinus
Size: To 40 in. (1 m)

Description: Highly variable in color, it is often gray to brownish above and has pink to red spots on its back and sides. Caudal fin is slightly forked with a yellowish border.

Habitat: Lakes and large rivers.

Comments: Closely related to lake trout and salmon, it tastes like a cross between the two.

MOUNTAIN WHITEFISH
Prosopium williamsoni
Size: To 28 in. (70 cm)

Description: Slender, silvery fish has a short head and a small mouth.

Habitat: Common in alpine lakes and streams.

Comments: A Colorado native. The smoked meat is considered a delicacy.

CHANNEL CATFISH
Ictalurus punctatus
Size: To 4 ft. (1.2 m)

Description: Olive to blue-gray catfish has dark spots scattered on its back and sides, prominent barbels (whiskers) and a forked tail.

Habitat: Warmer rivers and reservoirs.

Comments: A popular food and game fish. Native to eastern Colorado, it is stocked throughout the state.

LARGEMOUTH BASS
Micropterus salmoides
Size: To 38 in. (95 cm)

Description: Greenish, mottled fish with a dark, often blotched, side stripe. Has a large mouth with the upper jaw extending past the eye.

Habitat: Quiet, vegetated lakes, ponds and rivers.

Comments: Introduced to Colorado in 1878, this aggressive predatory sport fish is renowned for its fighting ability.

SMALLMOUTH BASS
Micropterus dolomieu
Size: To 27 in. (68 cm)

Description: Similar to the largemouth, it has blotched sides. Note that jaw margin does not extend beyond the eye.

Habitat: Warm and cool streams, lakes, reservoirs.

Comments: Prefers cooler, deeper water than the largemouth bass.

WIPER
Morone saxatilis x Morone chrysops
Size: To 20 in. (50 cm)

Description: Silvery fish has 6–9 broken side stripes.

Habitat: Ponds, rivers, lakes.

Comments: Hybrid between a striped bass and a white bass, it is a very popular, hard-fighting sport fish. An excellent table fish.

BLUEGILL
Lepomis macrochirus
Size: To 16 in. (40 cm)

Description: Flattened brassy fish with long pectoral fins and a dark-spotted dorsal fin. Dusky side bars are often present.

Habitat: Quiet, vegetated lakes, ponds and rivers.

Comments: One of the most popular sport fishes in the country, it is often stocked in lakes and impoundments.

GREEN SUNFISH
Lepomis cyanellus
Size: To 12 in. (30 cm)
Description: Has large mouth and dark spot on rear of second dorsal and anal fin.
Habitat: Clear ponds and streams with little current. Can tolerate turbid waters.
Comments: Widely introduced throughout Colorado, it weighs up to 2.2 lbs. (1 kg).

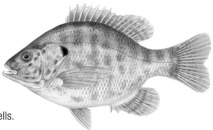

REDEAR SUNFISH
Lepomis microlophus
Size: To 14 in. (35 cm)
Description: Key field mark is black ear flap rimmed in red or orange.
Habitat: Clear, quiet ponds, lakes and streams.
Comments: Also called shellcracker, it has specialized teeth that help it to crack mollusk shells.

BLACK CRAPPIE
Pomoxis nigromaculatus
Size: To 20 in. (50 cm)
Description: Greenish, mottled fish with dorsal fin set well back on its hunched back. First of two dorsal fins has 7–8 stiff spines.
Habitat: Quiet, clear lakes, ponds and rivers.
Comments: Also tolerant of silty water, it is caught in a wide range of habitats. Can see well in the dark and is most active feeding in the evening. Often schools around vertical structures.

WHITE CRAPPIE
Pomoxis annularis
Size: To 20 in. (50 cm)
Description: Has a humped back, 6 dorsal spines, 6–9 dark side blotches and a white belly.
Habitat: Sandy or muddy bottomed streams and ponds, often in turbid water.
Comments: Is more tolerant of turbid water than the black crappie.

YELLOW PERCH
Perca flavescens
Size: To 16 in. (40 cm)
Description: Golden to brown fish with 6–9 dark side patches (saddles). Note black blotching at back of first dorsal fin.
Habitat: Clear streams, ponds and lakes.
Comments: Stocked in a number of lakes, it is a popular sport and food fish.

WALLEYE
Sander vitreus
Size: To 40 in. (1 m)

Description: Slender, dark fish with large fins, a huge mouth and a white spot on the bottom of its tail fin. Dark blotching is evident at the rear of the first dorsal fin.

Habitat: Warm- and cool-water reservoirs.

Comments: Named for its opaque, glassy eyes. Introduced to Colorado in 1949, it is a prized table fish and can reach weights in excess of 18 lbs. (8 kg).

SAUGER
Sander canadensis
Size: To 30 in. (75 cm)

Description: Bronze to brown cylindrical fish has 3–4 dark side saddles, a spotted dorsal fin and lacks white marks on the tail. Forked tail has pale streaks.

Habitat: Large rivers and lakes, often in turbid waters.

Comments: Has excellent night vision and is most active feeding at dusk, dawn and during the night.

SAUGEYE
Sander vitreus x
Sander canadensis
Size: 12–18 in. (30–45 cm)

Description: A mottled, dark fish, it has black pigmentation in between its dorsal fin spines and lacks a white tail spot.

Habitat: Reservoirs, lakes.

Comments: A walleye/sauger hybrid, it is a smaller version of its kin. Like its kin, it feeds almost exclusively on fish and is an excellent table fish.

TIGER MUSKIE
Esox lucius x
Esox masquinongy
Size: To 38 in. (95 cm)

Description: Large, torpedo-shaped fish has dark blotches on its back and a posterior dorsal fin. Large mouth is filled with teeth.

Habitat: Lakes, rivers and large reservoirs with abundant vegetation.

Comments: A hybrid of northern pike and muskie, it was introduced into Colorado in the 1980s in order to control the spread of suckers and carp. Weighs up to 50 lbs. (23 kg).

NORTHERN PIKE
Esox lucius
Size: To 52 in. (1.3 m)
Description: Elongate greenish
fish has large head and posterior dorsal fin.
Sides are covered with bean-shaped spots.
Habitat: Slow-moving streams and lakes with
abundant vegetation.
Comments: Voracious predator feeds primarily on fish but
will eat any animal it can swallow. Also called jackfish, it is
the most widely distributed North American fish.

PROTECTED SPECIES

These fishes can be found throughout the Colorado River Basin. If hooked, they must
be returned to the water unharmed as quickly as possible.

HUMPBACK CHUB
Gila cypha
Size: To 20 in. (50 cm)
Description: Greeenish to silvery fish
has a prominent bump behind the head.

BONYTAIL CHUB
Gila elegans
Size: To 2 ft. (60 cm)
Description: Note bump behind
head and long narrow tail.

RAZORBACK SUCKER
Xyrauchen texanus
Size: To 3 ft. (90 cm)
Description: Bronze to yellow fish has
a prominent bump behind the head.

COLORADO PIKEMINNOW
Ptychocheilus lucius
Size: To 60 in. (1.5 m)
Description: Greenish-gray to bronze
fish has whitish sides and belly.

IT IS ILLEGAL TO TAKE OR USE any of the following species from Colorado waters: Arkansas
darter, blueheadsucker, bonytail chub, boreal toad, brassy minnow, Colorado pikeminnow, common
shiner, flannelmouth sucker, flathead chub, greenback cutthroat trout, humpback chub, Iowa darter,
lake chub, mountain sucker, northern redbelly dace, plains minnow, plains topminnow, plains
orangethroat darter, razorback sucker, Rio Grande chub, Rio Grande sucker, river shiner, roundtail
chub, southern redbelly dace, stonecat, suckermouth minnow.

Butterflies and moths belong to the second largest order of insects (next to beetles) with approximately 170,000 species worldwide. All have two pairs of wings covered with overlapping layers of fine scales. They feed by uncoiling a long feeding-tube (proboscis) and sucking nutrients from flowers, puddles, etc. When not in use, the tube is coiled under the head.

The two groups differ in several ways:

BUTTERFLIES

- Active by day
- Brightly colored
- Thin body
- Rests with wings held erect over its back
- Antennae are thin and thickened at the tip

MOTHS

- Active at night
- Most are dull colored
- Stout body
- Rests with wings folded, tent-like, over its back
- Antennae are usually thicker and often feathery

All butterflies and moths have a complex life cycle consisting of four developmental stages.

1. **Eggs** – Eggs are laid singly or in clusters on vegetation or on the ground. One or more clutches of eggs may be laid each year.
2. **Caterpillars (larvae)** – These worm-like creatures hatch from eggs and feed primarily on plants (often on the host plant on which the eggs were laid). As they grow, larvae shed their skin periodically.
3. **Pupae** – Pupae are the 'cases' within which caterpillars transform into adults. The pupa of a butterfly is known as a chrysalis; those of moths are called cocoons. In cooler regions, pupae often over-winter before maturing into butterflies or moths.
4. **Adult** – Butterflies/moths emerge from pupae to feed and breed.

ATTRACTING BUTTERFLIES TO YOUR YARD

Food – Almost all butterfly caterpillars eat plants; adult butterflies feed almost exclusively on plant nectar. Your library or local garden shop will have information on which plants attract specific species.

Water – Soak the soil in your garden or sandy areas to create puddles. These provide a source of water and minerals.

Rocks – Put large flat rocks in sunny areas. Butterflies will gather there to spread their wings and warm up.

Brush – Small brush piles and hollow logs provide ideal places for butterflies to lay their eggs and hibernate over the winter.

SWALLOWTAILS & ALLIES

Family includes the largest butterfly species. Most are colorful and have a tail-like projection on each hindwing. All measurements denote wingspan unless otherwise noted.

BLACK SWALLOWTAIL

Papilio polyxenes – To 3.5 in. (9 cm)
Black to blue-black butterfly is yellow spotted and has bluish markings and orange eyespots near the rear of the hindwing.

TWO-TAILED SWALLOWTAIL

Pterourus multicaudatus – To 5 in. (13 cm)
The largest western butterfly has twin tails on each hindwing.

ANISE SWALLOWTAIL

Papilio zelicaon – To 3 in. (8 cm)
Note round, orange eyespot with a dark pupil. Found in variable habitats (excluding dense forests) to 14,000 ft. (4200 m).

WESTERN TIGER SWALLOWTAIL

Papilio rutulus – To 4 in. (10 cm)
One of the most familiar butterflies in Colorado, it is found along roadsides, in mountain woodlands and urban gardens.

PALE TIGER SWALLOWTAIL

Pterourus eurymedon – To 4 in. (10 cm)
The only black and white swallowtail found in the west. Found in mountainous and hilly areas from prairies to the timberline.

PHOEBUS PARNASSIAN

Parnassius phoebus – To 3 in. (8 cm)
Red-spotted cream to snow-white butterfly. Flies slowly and close to the ground in mountain woodlands and rocky areas at higher elevations.

WHITES & SULPHURS

White and yellow/orange butterflies are among the first to appear in spring.

COMMON SULPHUR

Colias philodice – To 2 in. (5 cm)
Bright yellow butterfly has dark wing margins,
a single spot near the top of each forewing and
a hindwing spot trimmed with red.

ORANGE SULPHUR

Colias eurytheme – To 2.5 in. (6 cm)
Bright gold-orange butterfly has dark to pinkish
wing margins and prominent forewing spots.

SARA ORANGETIP

Anthocharis sara – To 1.5 in. (4 cm)
White butterfly has bright orange wing tips.

CABBAGE WHITE

Pieris rapae – To 2 in. (5 cm)
Small, milk-white butterfly has four dark
spots on its forewings and hindwings.

SKIPPERS

Family of orange, brown and black butterflies are named for their fast, bouncing flight.
Most have distinctive antennae that end in curved clubs.

Underwings

SILVER-SPOTTED SKIPPER

Epargyreus clarus – To 2.5 in. (6 cm)
Medium-sized brown butterfly has a large, irregular
silver patch on the underside of its hindwings and
yellowish spots across the middle of the forewing.

COMMON CHECKERED SKIPPER

Pyrgus communis – To 1.25 in. (3.2 cm)
Extremely variable checkered white
and black to dark brown butterfly.

GOSSAMER-WINGED BUTTERFLIES

Family of small butterflies that often have small, hair-like tails on their hindwings. Many rest with their wings folded and underwings exposed.

SPRING AZURE

Celastrina ladon – To 1.25 in. (3.2 cm)
Bright pale blue butterfly is widespread and common in woodlands, roadsides and brushy areas at all elevations.

Colorado's
State Insect

COLORADO HAIRSTREAK

Hypaurotis crysalus – To 1.5 in. (4 cm)
Deep purple wings have golden orange spots. Hindwing has a white stripe near the base. Found in canyons and foothills between 5,000–7,000 ft. (1500–2100 m).

PURPLISH COPPER

Epidemia helloides – To 1.5 in. (4 cm)
Dull copper brown wings have a purplish sheen that is most evident in bright sunlight. Forewings have dark spots.

MELISSA BLUE

Lycaeides melissa – To 1.25 in. (3.2 cm)
Wings are vivid blue to dark blue and have narrow black margins. Found in open, sunny areas and dry mountain meadows.

TAILED BLUE

Cupido spp. – To 1.25 in. (3.2 cm)
Bright lavender blue wings have white margins. Note orange spots near tail on hindwing (often absent). Found in meadows, canyons, fields and forest margins.

Underwings

GRAY HAIRSTREAK

Strymon melinus – To 1.25 in. (3.2 cm)
Dark grayish underwings have bold orange and blue patches above tail. Upperwings are blue-gray.

BRUSHFOOT BUTTERFLIES

Named for their small hairy forelegs that they use to 'taste' food.

MILBERT'S TORTOISESHELL

Aglais milberti – To 2 in. (5 cm)

Wings are black with wide orange subterminal bands that fade to yellow at the inner edge.

WEIDEMEYER'S ADMIRAL

Limenitis weidemeyerii – To 3.5 in. (9 cm)

Large coal-black wings are covered by broad white bands. Found along waterways, sand hills, parklands and gardens.

MONARCH

Danaus plexippus – To 4 in. (10 cm)

Large cinnamon-orange butterfly has dark veins and rows of white spots on black wing margins. Found in meadows, fields and other open habitats.

VICEROY

Limenitis archippus – To 3 in. (8 cm)

Similar to the monarch but smaller, it has a thin black band on its hindwings. Believed to mimic the monarch because it is noxious to predators.

COMMON WOOD NYMPH

Cercyonis pegala – To 3 in. (8 cm)

Large brown butterfly has 2 eyespots on the forewing and 1–2 on the hindwing. Found in open woodlands, fields, meadows, along waterways and roadsides.

MOURNING CLOAK

Nymphalis antiopa – To 3.5 in. (9 cm)

Rich brown-maroon wings are bordered by a cream-yellow band and blue submarginal spots. Found along waterways and in glades, gardens, open fields and city parks.

EDWARD'S FRITILLARY

Speyeria edwardsii – To 3.5 in. (9 cm)
Tawny brown butterfly has black-bordered
wings with a margin of white and yellow
spots. Female lays eggs on violets, the
host plant for its caterpillars.

VARIEGATED FRITILLARY

Euptoieta claudia – To 3 in. (8 cm)
Tawny orange butterfly has upperwings with
thick, dark veins and black spots near margins.
Note zigzag band in the middle of both wings.

RED ADMIRAL

Vanessa atalanta – To 2.5 in. (6 cm)
Dark butterfly has prominent orange-red
to vermilion bars on forewings and on
hindwing border. Note white spots at apex
of forewings. Also called alderman.

APHRODITE FRITILLARY

Speyeria aphrodite – To 3 in. (8 cm)
Orange-brown wings are covered in black markings
including a row of dark chevrons along the wing
edges. Underwings are orange with many silvery
spots. Found in open areas and along woodland
edges in wet and dry habitats.

SATYR COMMA

Polygonia satyrus – To 2.5 in. (6 cm)
Tawny golden wings are covered in
black blotches and have ragged margins.
Found in clearings, valley bottoms, along
waterways, open woodlands and marshes.

HOARY COMMA

Polygonia gracilis – To 1.5 in. (4 cm)
Rusty-orange and black butterfly has
very ragged wing margins. Underwings
are frosty white on the outer half and
there is a silver comma-shaped mark at
the center of the hindwing.

PAINTED LADY

Vanessa cardui – To 3 in. (8 cm)
Salmon-orange wings are covered in black blotches. Forewing tips have white spots. Found in meadows, parks, mountains, disturbed areas. Favorite host plants include thistles and legumes. Also called thistle butterfly and cosmopolite.

BUCKEYE

Junonia coenia – To 2.5 in. (6 cm)
Tawny to dark brown butterfly has wings with scalloped edges. Note orange forewing bars and eight distinct eyespots. The eyespots are believed to scare off predators.

NORTHERN CRESCENT

Phyciodes cocyta – To 1.5 in. (4 cm)
Orange-brown butterfly has dark wing margins. Males' antennal clubs are orange. Found in moist open areas in rocky and wooded areas and along waterways. Host plants include sunflowers and asters.

HACKBERRY EMPEROR

Asterocampa celtis – To 2.5 in. (6 cm)
Brown to gray-brown butterfly has dark forewing tips with white spots and a single black eyespot lacking a pupil. Hackberry trees are the only host plant for this species.

GORGONE CHECKERSPOT

Chlosyne gorgone – To 1.8 in. (4.6 cm)
Orange butterfly has black wing markings. Note submarginal row of black dots. Found in open areas including hardwood forests, prairies, ridges, fields and along waterways. Favorite host plants include sunflowers.

COMMON ALPINE

Erebia epipsodea – To 2 in. (5 cm)
Dark brown butterfly has rounded wings with red-orange patches or bands with dark eyespots with white "pupils." Common at upper elevations in meadows, marshes, grassy fields and open forests.

CATERPILLARS

Tiger Swallowtail

Black Swallowtail

Cabbage White

Anise Swallowtail

Buckeye

Monarch

Mourning Cloak

Viceroy

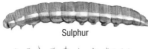
Sulphur

Skipper

Painted Lady

Tailed Blue

Tent Caterpillar

Red Admiral

Banded Woollybear

Five-spotted Hawkmoth

Imperial Moth

White-lined Sphinx

Webworm Caterpillar

Io Moth

MOTHS

POLYPHEMUS MOTH

Antheraea polyphemus – To 6 in. (15 cm)
Large, tan-colored moth has two yellow
forewing eyespots and two yellow hindwing
eyespots surrounded by blue and black. Males
have bushy antennae. Found in deciduous
forests, its host plants include hickory, birch,
walnut, beech and fruit trees.

FALL
WEBWORM MOTH

Hyphantria cunea –
To 1.5 in. (4 cm)
Wings are white with small dark
spots. Larvae are pests that attack
over 100 species of deciduous
trees and create webbed nests
over the branches and leaves in
late summer and fall.

Webworm Web

IMPERIAL MOTH

Eacles imperialis – To 7 in. (18 cm)
Yellow wings have pinkish-brown
to purplish-brown marks and brown
speckles. Host plants include pines,
maples, oaks, spruce and sweetgum.

HUMMINGBIRD CLEARWING

Hemaris thysbe – To 2 in. (5 cm)
Olive to burgundy above, it is instantly recognized
by its wings that have transparent patches. When
it hovers near flowers its wings make a buzzing
sound like a hummingbird. Found in meadows,
gardens and along forest edges.

BANDED WOOLLYBEAR

Pyrrharctia isabella – To 2 in. (5 cm)
Dull yellow to orangish above with sparse
black spotting, they have small heads and
bright red-orange forelegs. Named for the
appearance of the caterpillar (see p. 103),
they will roll up into balls when disturbed.
Also called Isabella tiger moth.

MILLER MOTH

Euxoa auxiliaris – To 1.5 in. (4 cm)
A seasonal nuisance in Colorado, large
populations migrate from low-lying farmlands
to the mountains each spring invading homes
and cars. At night, attracted by lights, they enter
homes and garages by the dozens each day of
migration. Also called army cutworm moths.

AMERICAN TENT CATERPILLAR MOTH

***Malacosoma americanum* –**
To 1.5 in. (4 cm)

Stout, furry moth has brown to gray forewings crossed by two light bands. Caterpillar is orange-brown with blue dots on its sides and back. When the larvae hatch in spring, they weave silken 'tents' between the branches of trees. Considered pests, the caterpillars often defoliate and kill the host tree.

Tent Caterpillar Web

WHITE-LINED SPHINX

***Hyles lineata* –** To 3.5 in. (9 cm)

Stout, furry moth has white stripes on the forewings and a thick pink stripe on the hindwings. Caterpillar has a red 'horn' at its rear. Active at all hours, it hovers like a hummingbird near flowers.

♀

IO MOTH

***Automeris io* –** To 3 in. (8 cm)

Male forewings are yellowish, females are red-brown. Hindwings have prominent eyespots ringed with black-blue and yellow. Female is brownish. Male is yellowish. Caterpillar spines can cause painful stings.

FIVE-SPOTTED HAWKMOTH

***Manduca quinquemaculata* –** To 5.5 in. (14 cm)

Torpedo-shaped grayish moth has wings streaked with zigzag black and brown lines. The caterpillar – often referred to as tomato hornworm – has a large horn at its rear. These are a major agricultural pest since they feed on tomato, potato, eggplant and pepper plants.

ACREA MOTH

***Estigmene acraea* –** To 2.8 in. (7 cm)

Head and thorax are white, abdomen is yellow-orange with 4–6 black spots. Found in fields, pastures and marshes. Caterpillar host plants include apple trees, cabbage, clover, corn, cotton, peas, potato, tobacco and other plants.

WESTERN SHEEPMOTH

***Hemileuca eglanterina* –** To 3.5 in. (9 cm)

Coloration is variable but forewings are typically pinkish and hindwings are yellowish. Black stripes and dots are prominent. Adults fly by day close to the ground. Is often found associated with livestock. Found at elevations to 8,400 ft. (2520 m).

TREES

Trees can be broadly defined as perennial woody plants at least 16 ft. (5 m) tall with a single stem and a well-developed crown of branches, twigs and leaves. Most are long-lived plants and range in age from 40–50 years for smaller deciduous trees to several hundred years for many of the conifers.

A tree's size and shape is largely determined by its genetic makeup, but growth is also affected by environmental factors such as moisture, light and competition from other species. Trees growing in crowded stands will often only support compact crowns due to the competition for light. Some species at high altitudes grow gnarled and twisted as a result of exposure to high winds.

Common Tree Silhouettes

| Pine | Juniper | Willow | Oak | Cottonwood |

SHRUBS

Shrubs are perennial woody plants normally less than 16 ft. (5 m) tall that support a crown of branches, twigs and leaves. Unlike trees, they are anchored to the ground by several stems rather than a single trunk. Most are fast-growing and provide an important source of food and shelter for wildlife.

N.B. – Some shrubs that are most conspicuous when in bloom are included in the section on flowering plants.

CACTI

This category includes a diverse array of desert and subtropical plants including palms, yuccas and cacti. Many are widely cultivated and common in urban settings. Palms and yuccas have leaves, whereas cacti have spines instead of leaves. Most are evergreen.

How to Identify Trees and Shrubs

First, note its size and shape. Does it have one or several 'trunks'? Examine the size, color and shape of the leaves and how they are arranged on the twigs. Are they opposite or alternate? Simple or compound? Hairy or smooth? Are flowers or fruits visible on branches or on the ground? Once you've collected as much information as you can, consult the illustrations and text to confirm your sighting.

SIMPLE LEAF SHAPES

| Elliptical | Heart-shaped | Rounded | Oval | Lobed | Lance-shaped |

COMPOUND LEAVES

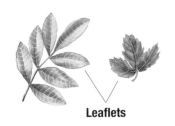

Leaflets

LEAF ARRANGEMENTS

Alternate **Opposite** **Whorled**

COMMON FRUITS

| **Drupe** | **Pome** | **Nut** | **Berry** |
| junipers, cherries, dogwoods, hollies | apples, plums, yuccas, pears | walnuts, pecans, hickories | blackberries, raspberries |

| **Winged Seed** | **Samara** | **Acorn** | **Pod** |
| dandelions, milkweeds, poplars, cottonwoods | maples, ashes, hophornbeams, elms | oaks | peas, mesquites, locusts |

PINES

Most have long, needle-like leaves that grow grouped in bundles of two to five. They lack true flowers and the seeds develop in the cones. Male and female cones usually occur on the same tree.

ROCKY MOUNTAIN BRISTLECONE PINE
Pinus aristata

Size: 15–40 ft. (4.5–12 m)

Description: Needles are arranged in tight bundles of 5 that grow curved around the twig. Purplish cones bristle with stiff, recurved prickles.

Habitat: Dry, rocky exposed slopes in central Colorado from 9,200–11,800 ft. (2760–3540 m).

Comments: The oldest living trees on earth, one Colorado specimen was estimated to be 2,480 years old. Often gnarled and twisted by high winds, they are often the only trees at the treeline.

LODGEPOLE PINE
Pinus contorta

Size: 65–80 ft. (20–24 m)

Description: Crown is ragged and slender, straight trunk is often barren when shaded. Stiff needles are twisted into bundles of 2. Cone scales have a single prickle near their outer edge.

Habitat: Bogs, alpine forests, sandy soils 5,000–12,000 ft. (1500–3600 m).

Comments: Named for its straight trunk, which Native Americans used for teepee poles. Cones are stimulated to open by heat and this is often one of the first trees to reseed burned-out areas after forest fires.

COLORADO PINYON PINE
Pinus edulis

Size: 15–45 ft. (4.5–13.5 m)

Description: Small, often shrubby, pine with spreading, rounded branches. Stiff, light green needles grow in 2's along twigs. Short-stalked, rounded cones produce large seeds.

Habitat: Dry, gravelly and rocky soils 5,200–9,000 ft. (1560–2700 m).

Comments: A very important wildlife tree, each cone contains up to 20 large, oily edible seeds that are eaten by birds, squirrels, porcupines, bears and deer.

LIMBER PINE
Pinus flexilis
Size: 40–50 ft. (12–15 m)

Description: Needles occur in stiff bundles of 5 and are clustered near the ends of branches. Large cones are up to 8 in. (20 cm) long.

Habitat: Dry, rocky ridges 5,000–12,000 ft. (1500–3600 m).

Comments: Named for its flexible, tough twigs. Grows prostrate in exposed locations and resembles a large, spreading shrub.

PONDEROSA PINE
Pinus ponderosa
Size: 50–160 ft. (15–48 m)

Description: Stout, stiff needles 5–8 in. (13–20 cm) long and grouped in bundles of 2–3. Oval cones have scales that terminate in sharp prickles.

Habitat: Dry, rocky ridges 6,300–9,500 ft. (1890–2850 m).

Comments: Widespread in mountain regions, often in pure stands, it grows in association with Douglas-fir, juniper and spruce.

SPRUCES

Relatively large evergreens found in the mountains, they are easily distinguished by their four-sided needles that grow from woody pegs along the branches. It is much easier to roll a spruce needle between your fingers than the two-sided needles of other evergreens. Profile is straight and tall.

COLORADO BLUE SPRUCE
Picea pungens
Size: 70–115 ft. (21–35 m)

Description: Diamond shaped needles are very prickly. Cones up to 4 in. (10 cm) long have irregularly toothed, ragged scales.

Habitat: Well drained, sandy soils 6,700–11,500 ft. (2010–3450 m).

Comments: Known for its stately, symmetrical form. Ranges in color from green to blue to silver and is also called the silver spruce.

Colorado's State Tree

ENGELMANN SPRUCE
Picea engelmannii
Size: 45–130 ft. (13–33 m)

Description: Trunk typically supports a compact conical crown of short branches. Needles have sharp tips and exude a skunk-like odor when crushed. Ragged cones (2 in./5 cm long) are pendant and often grow in clusters.

Habitat: Moist soils in the mountains 8,000–11,000 ft. (2400–3300 m).

Comments: Often grow in mixed stands with subalpine fir, Douglas-fir, limber pine and other conifers.

FIRS

Firs are medium-sized evergreens with dense, symmetrical crowns. Cones grow upright from branches and disintegrate when seeds are ripe. After the cone scales are shed, a central candle-like stalk remains on the branch.

SUBALPINE FIR
Abies lasiocarpa
Size: 60–100 ft. (18–30 m)

Description: Evergreen needles grow curved upward on twigs. Upright cone is purplish and 2–4 in. (5–10 cm) long.

Habitat: Rocky soils 8,000–12,000 ft. (2400–3600 m).

Comments: Also called Rocky Mountain fir, it grows in association with Engelmann spruce and other conifers.

WHITE FIR
Abies concolor
Size: 60–120 ft. (18–36 m)

Description: Flattened needles have white lines on both sides and grow curved upward. Barrel-shaped cones are up to 5 in. (13 cm) long and have fan-shaped scales.

Habitat: Moist soils 8,000–10,000 ft. (2400–3000 m).

Comments: Due to its straight profile and soft needles, it is a popular ornamental and Christmas tree.

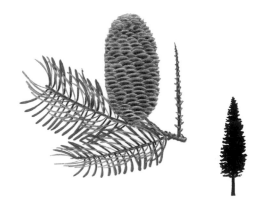

DOUGLAS-FIRS

Larger than true firs, Douglas-firs are easily identified by their shaggy cones.

DOUGLAS-FIR
Pseudotsuga menziesii
Size: 100–130 ft. (30–39 m)

Description: Flexible needles grow along twigs that terminate in red buds. Cones are distinguished at a glance by the 3-pointed bracts protruding between scales. Branches often droop.

Habitat: Moist, well-drained soils 6,000–9,500 ft. (1800–2850 m)

Comments: One of the tallest and most important timber trees in the U.S., coastal specimens reach up to 330 ft. (100 m).

JUNIPERS

All have scale-like or awl-shaped leaves that are tightly bunched on twigs. Branchlets are four-sided. Cones are composed of woody scales.

ROCKY MOUNTAIN JUNIPER
Juniperus scopulorum
Size: 15–50 ft. (4.5–15 m)

Description: Shrub or small tree. Leaves are small and scale-like and grow in whorls along twigs. Juicy, bluish berries normally contain 2–3 seeds.

Habitat: Rocky soils in the foothills and on the plains 5,000–9,000 ft. (1500–2700 m).

Comments: Specimens of this hardy plant live up to 1,500 years.

MAPLES

Maples are distinguished by their large, opposite-growing, lobed leaves and long-winged seed pairs (samaras).

BOXELDER
Acer negundo
Size: To 35 ft. (10.5 m)

Description: Leaves are up to 4 in. (10 cm) long and have 3–5 leaflets. Seeds are encased in paired, V-shaped papery keys.

Habitat: Wet soils in riparian areas and floodplains, disturbed sites.

Comments: Also called ash-leaf maple.

ROCKY MOUNTAIN MAPLE
Acer glabrum

Size: 20–30 ft. (6–9 m)

Description: Shrub or small tree. Leaves are up to 5 in. (13 cm) long and have reddish stalks. Greenish flowers bloom in drooping clusters in spring, and are succeeded by winged seed pairs in late summer.

Habitat: Moist soils 3,000–10,000 ft. (900–3000 m).

Comments: The seeds are eaten by rodents and birds, deer browse on the twigs and leaves.

WILLOW FAMILY

Deciduous trees are rapidly-growing and relatively short-lived. Flowers bloom in long clusters (catkins) in spring and are succeeded by fruiting capsules. When ripe, these pods burst open and shed numerous cottony seeds in the wind.

TREMBLING ASPEN
Populus tremuloides

Size: To 70 ft. (21 m)

Description: Long, slender trunk supports a crown of spreading branches. Rounded leaves have long stems and the leaves rustle (tremble) in the slightest breeze. Leaves turn yellow in autumn.

Habitat: Well-drained soils in a variety of habitats.

Comments: Its twigs, leaves, catkins and bark are an important food source for wildlife.

NARROWLEAF COTTONWOOD
Populus angustifolia

Size: To 60 ft. (18 m)

Description: Narrow, lance-shaped leaves have serrated edges and pointy tips. Brownish fruiting capsules are up to 1 in. (3 cm) long.

Habitat: Wet soils near water 5,000–8,000 ft. (1500–2400 m).

Comments: In dry areas, cottonwoods indicate the presence of underground water.

PLAINS COTTONWOOD
Populus deltoides
Size: 33–100 ft. (10–30 m)

Description: Large, triangular leaves are up to 6 in. (18 cm) long. Flowers are succeeded by capsules containing seeds with cottony 'tails'.

Habitat: Floodplains, riparian areas, moist woodlands in eastern Colorado 3,500–6,500 ft. (1050–1950 m).

Comments: Often grows in pure stands or in association with willows and oaks.

PEACHLEAF WILLOW
Salix amygdaloides
Size: To 40 ft. (12 m)

Description: Narrow, finely saw-toothed leaves are up to 4 in. (10 cm) long. Reddish-yellow fruits shed their seeds in late spring or early summer.

Habitat: Riparian areas and wetlands 3,500–7,500 ft. (1050–2280 m).

Comments: Leaves are thought to resemble those of a peach (*Amygdalus*). Grows in association with cottonwoods and maples.

ALDERS

Leaves are commonly oval-shaped with toothed margins. Distinctive, cylindrical, woody cones (strobiles) disintegrate in the fall when ripe. All are fast-growing and short-lived.

MOUNTAIN ALDER
Alnus incana tenuifolia
Size: 15–40 ft. (4.5–12 m)

Description: Leaves are coarsely toothed and up to 5 in. (13 cm) long. Flowers bloom in long clusters and are succeeded by distinctive, cone-like woody fruits.

Habitat: Found on moist soils and along waterways 5,000–10,000 ft. (1500–3000 m).

Comments: Shrub or small tree often forms dense thickets. Also called gray alder, speckled alder and thinleaf alder.

ROSES & ALLIES

A variable family of trees and shrubs found throughout North America.

ALDERLEAF MOUNTAIN MAHOGANY
Cercocarpus montanus

Size: To 20 ft. (6 m)

Description: Shrub or small tree with a spreading crown. Toothed, evergreen leaves are elliptical with a narrow base. Yellowish flowers are succeeded by fruits with a feathery plume at the tip.

Habitat: Dry mountain slopes.

Comments: The term *cercocarpus* is derived from the Greek words for 'tail' and 'fruit'.

COMMON CHOKECHERRY
Prunus virginiana

Size: 5–30 ft. (1.5–9 m)

Description: Shrub or small tree. Cylindrical clusters of aromatic flowers are succeeded by dark, red-purple berries.

Habitat: Variable habitats from 5,000–10,000 ft. (1500–3000 m).

Comments: A primary source of fruits to early Native Americans, the berries were also believed to have medicinal properties. The leaves – which release cyanide when wilted – are toxic to many animals including deer, cattle and horses.

OAKS

Oaks represent a group of important hardwoods. Generally, they are large trees with stout trunks and spreading crowns that produce acorns for fruit.

GAMBEL OAK
Quercus gambelii

Size: 10–15 ft. (3–4.5 m)

Description: Small tree or a thicket-forming shrub. Distinctive leaves have 5–9 deep lobes and are up to 6 in. (15 cm) long. Acorns are broadly oval.

Habitat: Open areas in mountains and foothills 4,000–8,000 ft. (1200–2400 m).

Comments: Often grows in association with ponderosa pine and pinyon pine.

SHRUBS

This general grouping includes species from a multitude of families.

SMOOTH SUMAC
Rhus glabra
Size: To 20 ft. (6 m)
Description: Bark is gray and smooth. Pyramidical clusters of white flowers are succeeded by 'hairy' red fruits.
Habitat: Foothills, woodland edges and open areas.
Comments: The plant is easy to spot in the fall when its leaves turn brilliant red. Fruits persist into late fall and winter.

WAX CURRANT
Ribes cereum
Size: To 6 ft. (1.8 m)
Description: Leaves are fan- or kidney-shaped. Pinkish-white, tubular, 5-petalled flowers bloom in early spring and are succeeded by edible red berries.
Habitat: Rocky, dry areas in foothills, montane and subalpine habitats.
Comments: The term "cereum" means waxy for the waxy secretions made by the leaves. Berries are soft, juicy and fruity-tasting.

GREENLEAF MANZANITA
Arctostaphylos patula
Size: 3–6 ft. (.9–1.8 m)
Description: Erect, evergreen shrub has smooth reddish branches and oval leaves. Urn-shaped flowers bloom in drooping clusters and are succeeded by red, berry-like drupes.
Habitat: Wooded slopes in western Colorado from 1,500–12,000 ft. (450–3600 m).
Comments: Grows in association with ponderosa pine and Gambel oak, the fruits attract a wide variety of animals including bears (*Arcto* in Greek).

MOUNTAIN CURRANT
Ribes montigenum
Size: To 5 ft. (1.5 m)
Description: Hairy leaves have 5 toothed lobes and large horns at the leaf node. Bell-shaped flowers are pinkish and have stamens with yellow anthers and bloom in dense clusters. Edible fruits have dark hairs.
Habitat: Moist woodlands.
Comments: Also called mountain gooseberry and prickly currant.

BIG SAGEBRUSH
Artemisia tridentata
Size: 2–20 ft. (.6–6 m)
Description: Gray-green shrub or small tree with narrow, 3-toothed, wedge-shaped leaves. Inconspicuous yellowish flowers bloom at stem tips.
Habitat: Deserts, mountain slopes and plains.
Comments: Plant emits an aromatic sage odor when handled. Important food source for deer, grouse and livestock.

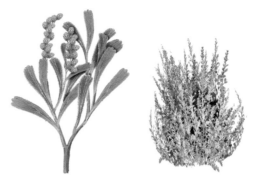

SERVICEBERRY
Amelanchier alnifolia
Size: 3–26 ft. (1–8 m)
Description: Shrub or small tree often grows in tickets. Oval, alternate leaves are coarsely toothed on upper half. White, star-shaped, 5-petalled flowers bloom June–July and are succeeded by purplish, sweet berries.
Habitat: Open woodlands, banks and hillsides from plains to montane region.
Comments: An important food source for early Native Americans, the fruits were eaten fresh, dried, mashed into cakes and used to flavor and preserve pemmican. Also called Saskatoon, Juneberry and shadbush.

RED-OSIER DOGWOOD
Cornus sericea

Size: 3–15 ft. (.9–4.5 m)

Description: Thicket-forming shrub. Opposite leaves are egg- to lance-shaped. White flowers bloom in summer and are succeeded by waxy white berries. Bark is reddish.

Habitat: Moist sites under 9,000 ft. (2700 m).

Comments: Often grows with willows and alders. Fruit is an important food source for grouse, deer, elk and rabbits.

BROOM SNAKEWEED
Gutierrezia sarothrae

Size: To 3 ft. (90 cm)

Description: Dense clusters of bright yellow ray flowers bloom at the end of smooth, brittle stems in summer. The lower leaves are often shed before the plant flowers. Crown is round and symmetrical.

Habitat: Semi-desert, roadsides, open areas, dry foothills.

Comments: The bushy stems die back during dormancy, giving the plant a broom-like appearance. Since cattle do not eat this plant, it often spreads over large areas

RABBITBRUSH
Ericameria nauseosa

Size: 3–7 ft. (.9–2.1 m)

Description: Small shrub with wiry, erect, hairy stems and small blue-green leaves. Terminal clusters of small yellow flowers bloom August–October.

Habitat: Dry plains, along slopes and washes.

Comments: An important food source for jackrabbits and deer. Often grows in association with sagebrush. Also called rubber rabbitbrush, it was considered a potential source of rubber in the early 1900s.

KINNIKINNICK
Arctostaphylos uva-ursi

Size: To 12 in. (30 cm)

Description: Evergreen shrub has shiny, spoon-shaped leaves that grow alternately along stems. Pinkish, bell-shaped flowers bloom in terminal clusters and are succeeded by red-orange, mealy berries that often persist into winter.

Habitat: Open woodlands from the foothills to alpine areas.

Comments: Also known as bearberry and pinemat manzanita, it often forms large mats.

GREASEWOOD
Sarcobatus vermiculatus

Size: To 5 ft. (1.5 m)

Description: Extremely thorny shrub has grayish bark and rich green succulent leaves. Female flowers are enclosed in cone-like structures. Greenish seed pods turn brownish with age.

Habitat: Open dry areas on fine-grained soils.

Comments: Plant was first collected in 1806 by the Lewis and Clark Expedition.

SHRUBBY CINQUEFOIL
Dasiphora fruticosa

Size: 3–5 ft. (90–150 cm)

Description: Small, woody plant has reddish, shredding bark and toothed leaves with 3–9 lobes. Buttercup-shaped, 5-petalled flowers bloom at the ends of stems June–August.

Habitat: Pastures, roadsides, hillsides, gardens, meadows from foothills to subalpine.

Comments: Widely cultivated as an ornamental, the plant is still widely referenced in horticultural literature by its former name (*Potentilla fruticosa*). Also called hardhack, shrubby five-finger and tundra rose.

BITTERBRUSH
Purshia tridentata

Size: To 6 ft. (1.8 m)

Description: Sprawling, unkempt evergreen shrub has three-lobed leaves. Fragrant flowers are rose-like. Easily identified by its fruits, which have 4-winged husks.

Habitat: Semi-desert, woodlands, shrublands from 1,000–3,000 ft. (300–900 m).

Comments: Blooms April–July. Also called antelopebrush.

POISON IVY
Toxicodendron spp.

Size: To 8 ft. (2.4 m)

Description: Shrub or vine has three-part leaves. The leaves are maroon-red when new, green as they mature and then turn scarlet in autumn. Flowers bloom in loose clusters May–July.

Habitat: Well-drained soils in woodlands.

Comments: These plants contain a toxic oil that causes minor to severe rashes and blistering on contact. Most severe reactions are caused by ingesting berries or breathing the smoke from burning plants.

SNOWBERRY
Symphoricarpos albus

Size: 2–6.5 ft. (.6–2 m)

Description: Opposite oval leaves have smooth edges. Pink to white, funnel-shaped flowers bloom in small clusters and are succeeded by waxy white berries that persist into autumn.

Habitat: Well-drained soils in open woodlands, plains to subalpine.

Comments: Blooms June–August. The branches, leaves and fruits are poisonous and early settlers referred to them as "corpse berries" or "snake's berries".

CACTI & ALLIES

These evergreens differ from other plants by having leaves with parallel veins and trunks that lack growth rings. Most have been introduced from the tropics.

CLARET CUP CACTUS
Echinocereus triglochidiatus
Size: 4–12 in. (10–30 cm)

Description: Mound-forming cactus grows in bulbous piles of up to several hundred individual stems. Showy, funnel-shaped, bright scarlet red to orange-red flowers bloom in spring.

Habitat: Deserts, mountain woodlands and rocky slopes between 1,500–10,000 ft. (45–3000 m).

Comments: Also called kingcup cactus, Mohave mound cactus and claretcup. The flowers are pollinated by hummingbirds.

Colorado's State Cactus

TREE CHOLLA
Cylindropuntia imbricata
Size: To 16 ft. (5 m)

Description: Shrubby to tree-sized cactus has interweaved thick branches that are heavily spined. Large, attractive, bell-shaped flowers have overlapping petals. Fruits are yellow.

Habitat: Rocky areas, shrublands 4,000–7,500 ft. (1200–2300 m).

Comments: Blooms May–July. Also called cane cholla, walking stick cholla and chainlink cactus.

GREEN PITAYA
Echinocereus viridiflorus
Size: To 10 in. (25 cm)

Description: Cactus has a single rounded or cylindrical stem. Flowers are yellow-green to reddish.

Habitat: Prairies, desert scrub, grasslands.

Comments: Also called small-flowered hedgehog cactus.

PRICKLY PEAR CACTUS
Opuntia phaeacantha

Size: Pads to 3 ft. (90 cm)

Description: A sprawling or erect cactus with jointed, prickly pads growing in dense clusters. Yellow flowers bloom April–June.

Habitat: Deserts, rangeland, waste areas.

Comments: One of several similar species of *Opuntia* found in Colorado. Both the fruit (tuna) and the pads are consumed by humans and wildlife.

SOAPWEED YUCCA
Yucca glauca

Size: To 4 ft. (1.2 m)

Description: Evergreen palm-like shrub or small tree with one or more trunks. Leaves are bayonet-like. Large, bell-shaped flowers bloom in a long terminal spike. Fruit is a dry capsule with shiny black seeds.

Habitat: Dry, rocky and gravelly slopes, sandy plains.

Comments: Native Americans used the plant as a food source by boiling the seed pods. The root was pounded and made into suds for washing. The leaves were used to make ropes, mats and brushes.

BLUE YUCCA
Yucca baccata

Size: To 5 ft. (1.5 m)

Description: Blue-green, sword-like leaves up to 40 in. (1 m) long. White to creamy flowers with purple shades bloom April–July.

Habitat: Pinyon-juniper and ponderosa pine forests, sagebrush plains between 5,000–8,200 ft. (1500–2500 m).

Comments: Also called banana yucca, its fruit is banana-shaped and was an important winter food source for Paiute Indians.

Wildflowers are soft-stemmed flowering plants, usually smaller than trees or shrubs, that grow anew each year. Some regenerate annually from the same rootstock (perennials), while others grow from seeds and last a single season (annuals). Most have flowering stems bearing colorful blossoms that ripen into fruits as the growing season progresses. The flowering stem typically grows upright, but may be climbing, creeping or trailing.

N.B. – This section covers wildflowers and includes some shrubs that are conspicuous when in bloom.

The species in this section have been grouped according to color rather than family to facilitate field identification. The color groups used are:

- White
- Yellow, Orange and Green
- Red and Pink
- Blue and Purple

How to Identify Wildflowers

After noting color, examine the shape of the flower heads. Are they daisy-like, bell-shaped, or cross-shaped? How are they arranged on the plant? Do they occur singly or in clusters? Are the flower heads upright or drooping? Pay close attention to the leaves and how they are arranged on the stem. Refer to the illustrations and text to confirm its size, habitat and blooming period.

N.B. – The blooming periods of flowers can vary depending on latitude, elevation and the weather. The dates given are meant to serve as general guidelines only.

Remember that flowers are wildlife and should be treated as such. Many species have been seriously depleted due to loss of habitat and overpicking. In many areas, once-abundant species are now rare. Bring along a sketchbook and camera to record the flowers you see instead of picking them. This will help ensure there are more blossoms for you and others to enjoy in years to come.

N.B. – It is illegal to collect most of Colorado's native plants. Check with the Department of Forestry regarding protected and endangered species.

FLOWER STRUCTURE

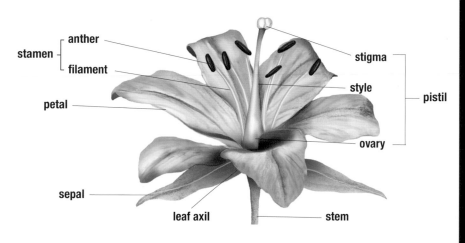

anther

stamen

filament

stigma

petal

style

pistil

sepal

ovary

leaf axil

stem

FLOWER SHAPES

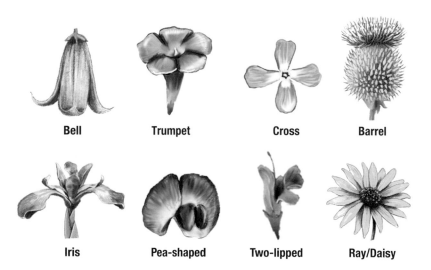

Bell	Trumpet	Cross	Barrel
Iris	Pea-shaped	Two-lipped	Ray/Daisy

WHITE FLOWERS

SEGO LILY
Calochortus nuttallii
Size: 8–18 in. (20–45 cm)

Description: Erect plant has unbranched stems and 1–4 showy, bell-shaped white flowers.

Habitat: Dry slopes, open plains.

Comments: Also called mariposa (butterfly) lily by early Spanish explorers for the plants' resemblance to fluttering butterflies on the open plains.

SNOWBALL SAXIFRAGE
Saxifraga rhomboidea
Size: 4–12 in. (10–30 cm)

Description: Erect plant has a hairy stem and a dense cluster of tiny white flowers. Diamond-shaped leaves grow in a basal cluster.

Habitat: Moist soils from the plains to high in the mountains.

Comments: Blooms May–August. Also called diamond leaf saxifrage.

YARROW
Achillea millefolium
Size: 6–20 in. (15–50 cm)

Description: A long, unbranched stem supports dense clusters of round, yellow-centered daisy-like flowers. Each flower has 4 to 6 white (occasionally pinkish) rays. The unusual fern-like leaves are a good field mark.

Habitat: Common in ditches, fields and disturbed areas near woodlands.

Comments: An aromatic herb, it is also known as milfoil and tansy. Blooms June–August.

PHLOX
Phlox spp.
Size: To 20 in. (50 cm)

Description: Five-petalled, yellow-centered flowers may be white, yellow, pink, red or lavender. Grows in sprawling clusters.

Habitat: Dry, open rocky areas.

Comments: Blooms April–July. Flowers have a sweet scent and are popular garden plants.

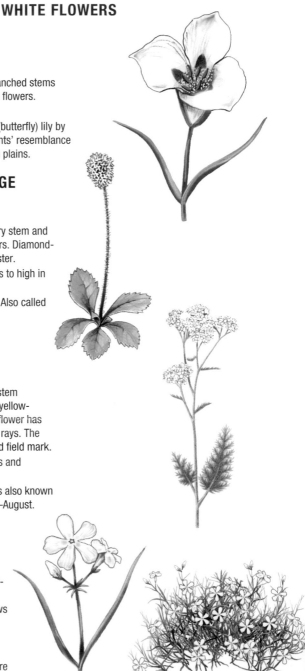

WILD CANDYTUFT
Thlaspi montanum

Size: To 10 in. (25 cm)

Description: Yellow-centered, white flowers bloom in a terminal cluster. One or several stems grow from a basal rosette of leaves.

Habitat: Open mountain slopes on thin soils.

Comments: Also called mountain candytuft, it blooms March–August.

DEATH CAMAS
Zigadenus elegans

Size: 6–28 in. (15–70 cm)

Description: Long basal leaves are grass-like. Star-shaped, green-centered flowers bloom in a long terminal cluster.

Habitat: Rocky slopes, mountain meadows.

Comments: Plant is highly poisonous to livestock and humans. Blooms June–August.

SINGLE DELIGHT
Moneses uniflora

Size: 2–6 in. (5–15 cm)

Description: Small plant is topped by a single, white to pink, saucer-shaped flower. Leaves grow in whorls of 3–4 near the plant base.

Habitat: Coniferous forests.

Comments: Also known as wood nymph and waxflower. Blooms May–August.

COW PARSNIP
Heracleum lanatum

Size: To 10 ft. (3 m)

Description: A large, conspicuous plant with deeply lobed leaves growing along the length of its thick, hollow stem. Dense, flattened clusters of creamy white flowers bloom March–September.

Habitat: Common in moist fields and woods.

Comments: Though non-poisonous, it resembles similar plants, like the water hemlock, which are deadly.

FIELD BINDWEED
Convolvulus arvensis
Size: 12–36 in. (30–90 cm)
Description: Long trailing stems have arrowhead-shaped leaves. White to pinkish, funnel-shaped flowers grow on short stalks.
Habitat: Fields, gardens, roadsides.
Comments: Very common, non-native species is widespread throughout North America.

WHITE MOUNTAIN AVENS
Dryas octopetala
Size: Creeping plant has stalks up to 10 in. (25 cm) long.
Description: Small, prostrate plant often grows in dense clusters. Leafless stalks support single flowers with 8–10 petals.
Habitat: Open rocky areas from middle elevations to the timberline.
Comments: Grows low to the ground to protect it from cold winds.

STEMLESS DAISY
Townsendia exscapa
Size: 1–2 in. (3–5 cm)
Description: Nearly stemless plant has a dense rosette of gray-green, hairy leaves. Solitary, yellow-centered flowerhead has numerous white to pinkish petals.
Habitat: Open areas on the plains and in juniper-pinyon woodlands.
Comments: Blooms March–May. Also called Easter daisy.

PEARLY EVERLASTING
Anaphalis margaritacea
Size: 8–36 in. (20–90 cm)
Description: Woolly stems are topped with dense, rounded clusters of creamy white flowers.
Habitat: Fields, roadsides, open woodlands.
Comments: Blooms June–September. Dried plants are often used in flower arrangements.

CRESTED PRICKLEPOPPY
Argemone polyanthemos
Size: 20–48 in. (.5–1.2 m)
Description: Blue-green, deeply lobed leaves are covered in yellow prickles. Delicate, papery white flowers have 4–6 petals.
Habitat: Sandy and gravelly soils, dry slopes, roadsides.
Comments: All parts of the plant are poisonous. Blooms April–July.

WHITE TRILLIUM
Trillium ovatum
Size: To 16 in. (40 cm)
Description: White, 3-petalled flower is framed by a whorl of 3 broad leaves.
Habitat: Forest floors, stream banks.
Comments: Arrives with the robin in spring, it is also referred to as western wake robin. Blooms February–June.

QUEEN ANNE'S LACE
Daucus carota
Size: 12–48 in. (30–120 cm)
Description: Plant with lacy foliage supports a large flat-topped cluster of tiny white flowers. Flower clusters become cup-shaped as they age.
Habitat: Fields, waste areas, roadsides.
Comments: Also called wild carrot, this introduced ancestor to the cultivated carrot blooms May–September.

WESTERN BISTORT
Polygonum bistortoides
Size: 8–28 in. (20–70 cm)
Description: Slender reddish stalk supports a dense cluster of white to pinkish flowers.
Habitat: Wet meadows, streamsides.
Comments: Also called knotweed, smokeweed and snakeweed. Blooms May–August and often covers mountain meadows.

OXEYE DAISY
Chrysanthemum leucanthemum
Size: 8–30 in. (20–90 cm)
Description: Dark green, leafy plant has stems topped by a single flowerhead with many white rays and a yellow center.
Habitat: Pastures, roadsides, fields.
Comments: Introduced species is widespread in Colorado. Blooms May–October.

WESTERN SPRING BEAUTY
Claytonia lanceolata
Size: 2–10 in. (5–25 cm)
Description: Small plant has two fleshy leaves. Small white to pinkish flowers often have dark veins.
Habitat: Moist soils from the foothills to high mountains.
Comments: Typically blooms April–July but has been known to appear as early as January. Thick underground root is a favorite of wildlife including bears and rodents.

MARSH MARIGOLD
Caltha leptosepala
Size: 3–10 in. (8–25 cm)
Description: Erect stems are topped by saucer-shaped flowers. Heart-shaped, shiny leaves have slightly scalloped edges.
Habitat: Found in mountain marshes and wet meadows, it is a favorite of elk and is also called elk's lip. Blooms May–August.

CANADA VIOLET
Viola canadensis
Size: 4–16 in. (10–40 cm)
Description: Short stalks support white flowers growing from the axils of heart-shaped leaves. White flower petals have yellowish bases that turn violet with age.
Habitat: Moist woodlands.
Comments: Blooms May–July.

WHITE VIRGIN'S BOWER
Clematis ligusticifolia
Size: Vine to 10 ft. (3 m)
Description: Woody vine is covered with hundreds of creamy white flowers.
Habitat: Riparian areas in forests and plains.
Comments: Blooms May–September. Also called pepper vine, pipestems and traveler's joy.

STAR-FLOWERED LILY-OF-THE-VALLEY
Maianthemum stellatum
Size: 12–24 in. (30–60 cm)
Description: Unbranched arching stem has lance- to oval-shaped alternate leaves. Tiny, star-shaped white flowers bloom in an elongate spray at the end of the stem.
Habitat: Moist woods (especially aspen), meadows and along streams.
Comments: Also known as starflower and false Solomon's seal. Blooms May–July.

AMERICAN GLOBEFLOWER
Trollius laxus albiflorus
Size: 4–20 in. (10–50 cm)
Description: One or more leafy stems is topped with a cup-shaped, greenish to white flower. Leaves have 5 toothed lobes.
Habitat: Wet areas in mountains.
Comments: Blooms May–August. Distinguished from the similar marsh marigold by its leaves.

RED BANEBERRY
Actaea rubra
Size: 2–3 ft. (60–90 cm)
Description: Compound leaves are thrice-divided and coarsely toothed. Flowers bloom in a dense, conical cluster and are succeeded by eye-catching poisonous red berries in summer.
Habitat: Cool shady deciduous and coniferous forests on well-drained soils.
Comments: Flower and seed heads often become so heavy the plant grows prostrate. Blooms May–July.

YELLOW & ORANGE FLOWERS

YELLOW STONECROP
Sedum lanceolatum
Size: 2–5 in. (5–13 cm)
Description: Small, succulent plant has waxy leaves to prevent water loss. Flowers bloom in erect clusters.
Habitat: Rocky soils from the plains to alpine zones.
Comments: Blooms June–August.

YELLOW SALSIFY
Tragopogon dubius
Size: 15–30 in. (38–75 cm)
Description: Branching hollow stems have grass-like leaves. Pale yellow flowerhead is distinctive.
Habitat: Roadsides, waste areas.
Comments: The flowers are succeeded by seed-like fruits covered in feathery brown bristles. Blooms May–September.

HEARTLEAF ARNICA
Arnica cordifolia
Size: 4–24 in. (10–60 cm)
Description: Stems have 2–4 pairs of heart-shaped leaves and are topped by 1–3 yellow flowerheads with numerous rays and yellow centers.
Habitat: Shady woodlands, roadsides.
Comments: Blooms April–September.

GOLDENROD
Solidago canadensis
Size: 1–6 ft. (.3–1.8 m)
Description: Tall, leafy plant with spreading, arched clusters of tiny yellow flowers. Leaves are hairy with three prominent veins.
Habitat: Meadows, pastures, open forests, waste areas.
Comments: One of several similar species found in Colorado. Widespread to the point that it is considered a nuisance in some areas. Blooms May–September.

SUNFLOWER
Helianthus spp.
Size: To 10 ft. (3 m)
Description: Tall, leafy plant with a branching stem supporting numerous yellow, dark-centered flowers.
Habitat: Roadsides, disturbed areas, open fields.
Comments: Flowers follow the sun across the sky each day. Blooms June–September.

YELLOW MONKEYFLOWER
Mimulus guttatus
Size: 10–36 in. (25–90 cm)
Description: Leafy plant has yellow, trumpet-shaped flowers with reddish spots near the blossom base.
Habitat: Wet areas.
Comments: Named for the monkey-like face on the flowers. Also called wild lettuce. Blooms May–August.

SULPHURFLOWER BUCKWHEAT
Eriogonum umbellatum
Size: 4–15 in. (10–38 cm)
Description: Erect stems support ball-like clusters of yellow to cream flowers on umbrella-like stalks.
Habitat: Dry areas from plains to mountains.
Comments: Also called umbrella plant. Blooms June–August.

WESTERN WALLFLOWER
Erysimum capitatum
Size: 6–36 in. (15–90 cm)
Description: Erect stems with narrow leaves support a showy cluster of yellow, orange or maroon-orange flowers.
Habitat: Dry, stony banks and slopes, open flats.
Comments: Named for the fact it grows near stone walls and rocks. Native Americans used its seeds to flavor food. Blooms July–August.

OREGON GRAPE
Mahonia repens

Size: 4–8 in. (10–20 cm)

Description: Leathery leaves have sharp, scalloped edges. Stems end in small clusters of yellow flowers that are succeeded by blue berries.

Habitat: Open woodlands.

Comments: The berries are an important food source for wildlife and also make a good jelly. Blooms March–June.

YELLOW CONEFLOWER
Ratibida columnifera

Size: 1–4 ft. (.3–1.2 m)

Description: Leaves have narrow segments. Flowerhead has 3–7 drooping rays surrounding a green-brown central disk.

Habitat: Prairies, roadsides, open areas.

Comments: Also called Mexican hat. Blooms July–October.

ARROWLEAF GROUNDSEL
Senecio triangularis

Size: 1–5 ft. (.3–1.5 m)

Description: Leaves are triangular or arrow-shaped. Leafy stems are topped by clusters of flowers with thin yellow rays.

Habitat: Streambanks and moist areas in the mountains.

Comments: Also called triangle-leaved ragwort. Blooms June–September.

BUFFALO GOURD
Cucurbita foetidissima

Size: Creeping plant has stems to 20 ft. (6 m) long

Description: Malodorous plant has large, triangular leaves growing along prostrate stems. Yellow, funnel-shaped flowers bloom May–August, often hidden beneath the leaves.

Habitat: Open areas on plains and deserts.

Comments: The fruit, a round, striped gourd about 3 in. (8 cm) wide, is very visible in winter. The mildly poisonous gourds are eaten by desert animals.

YELLOW MOUNTAIN DANDELION
Agoseris glauca
Size: 4–28 in. (10–70 cm)

Description: Narrow lance-shaped leaves are broader above the middle. Leafless stalks support large yellow flowerheads with numerous rays.

Habitat: Open areas in foothills, montane, subalpine and alpine regions.

Comments: One of several similar species of *Agoseris* found in Colorado.

INDIAN BLANKET
Gaillardia pulchella
Size: 1–2 ft. (30–60 cm)

Description: Branched leafy stems support fiery pinwheel-shaped flowers that have red rays tipped in yellow. Inner disk is maroon and dome-shaped.

Habitat: Sandy soils, disturbed areas, roadsides.

Comments: Also called firewheel, the flower's beauty inspired early Native American women to weave its colors into blankets. Conspicuous along roadsides, it often blankets large open areas. Blooms May–July.

GLACIER LILY
Erythronium grandiflorum
Size: 6–12 in. (15–30 cm)

Description: Two lance-shaped basal leaves frame a stalk supporting 1–5 golden flowers that have petal-like segments pulled back to expose the stamens.

Habitat: Mountain woodlands, sagebrush slopes, often near melting snow.

Comments: Also called dogtooth violet, yellow fawn lily and snow lily. Bulb is edible and is a food source for bears and rodents. Blooms March–August.

ARROWLEAF BALSAMROOT
Balsamorhiza sagittata
Size: 8–30 in. (20–75 cm)

Description: Has a basal cluster of arrow-shaped leaves covered in silvery hairs. The stem supports a single bright yellow flower with 8–25 rays.

Habitat: Grasslands, open woodlands.

Comments: Also called bigroot and big sunflower. Blooms May–July. The similar sunflower has several flowers atop each stem.

PARRY'S LOUSEWORT
Pedicularis parryi
Size: 4–12 in. (10–30 cm)

Description: Leaves are fern-like. Yellow-white flowers are beaked and seem to have two lips. **Habitat:** Open woodlands, meadows.

Comments: Is a member of the snapdragon (*Scrophulariaceae*) family. Blooms June–August.

BLANKETFLOWER
Gaillardia aristata
Size: 10–30 in. (25–75 cm)

Description: Light green leaves are elongate and hairy. Yellow rays surround a brown-maroon central disk.

Habitat: Open areas in the foothills and montane regions.

Comments: Also called gaillardia and brown-eyed Susan. Blooms May–September.

GOLDEN BANNER
Thermopsis spp.
Size: 2–4 ft. (60–120 cm)

Description: Hollow stems support elongated clusters of yellow, pea-like flowers. Leaves have 3 lance-shaped leaflets.

Habitat: Meadows, dry open areas.

Comments: Also called golden pea, buck bean and prairie goldbean. Blooms May–August.

ALPINE SUNFLOWER
Tetraneuris grandiflora
Size: 5–15 in. (13–38 cm)

Description: A low mat of leaves covered in cottony hairs supports sunflower-like flowers with three-toothed petals. Center disk turns from yellow to tan with age.

Habitat: Open, rocky alpine areas.

Comments: Also called old-man-of-the-mountain for its woolly appearance. Blooms June–July.

BLACK-EYED SUSAN
Rudbeckia hirta
Size: To 3 ft. (90 cm)
Description: Flowers have long yellow rays (often drooping) surrounding a brown to maroon, convex central disk.
Habitat: Waste areas, fields, meadows.
Comments: Stems and leaves are bristly to the touch.

WOOLLY MULLEIN
Verbascum thapsus
Size: To 7 ft. (2.1 m)
Description: Tall leafy plant that tapers from a broad base to a slender spike of yellow flowers. Flowers bloom a few at a time throughout summer.
Habitat: Fields, roadsides, waste areas.
Comments: Introduced invasive plant is very common. Miners used to make torches from these plants by dipping them in tallow.

SUBALPINE BUTTERCUP
Ranunculus eschscholtzii
Size: 2–10 in. (5–25 cm)
Description: Low-growing plants have flowers with 5–8 shiny brilliant yellow petals.
Habitat: Woodlands and meadows in alpine and subalpine areas.
Comments: One of several similar species of Colorado buttercups. Blooms June–August.

EVENING PRIMROSE
Oenothera spp.
Size: To 3 ft. (90 cm)
Description: Tall plant with long, slender leaves. Large, 4-petalled yellow flowers bloom June–September.
Habitat: Roadsides and grassy slopes from low to middle elevations.
Comments: As the common name suggests, the flowers open near the end of the day.

RED & PINK FLOWERS

SHOOTING STAR
Dodecatheon pulchellum
Size: To 20 in. (50 cm)

Description: Graceful plant with drooping, dart-like reddish flowers with inverted petals exposing yellow stamen tube.

Habitat: Moist soils in meadows, fields and open woodlands.

Comments: Blooms May–August. Related to primroses and cyclamens.

OLD MAN'S WHISKERS
Geum triflorum
Size: To 16 in. (40 cm)

Description: Reddish branched stalks support bell-shaped pinkish flowers. As the flowers age, the flowers turn upward and plumes begin to grow from the pistils to aid in seed dispersion.

Habitat: Sagebrush plains to mountain meadows.

Comments: Also known as prairie smoke and purple avens. Blooms April–August.

COWBOY'S DELIGHT
Sphaeralcea coccinea
Size: 10–20 in. (25–50 cm)

Description: Flowers are tomato-red or red-orange. Leaves are covered in fine hairs.

Habitat: Arid grasslands, pinyon-juniper woodlands.

Comments: Also called scarlet globemallow. A favorite of mule deer and bighorn sheep. Blooms June–August.

ALPINE PRIMROSE
Primula parryi
Size: To 15 in. (38 cm)

Description: Stout, leafless stalk supports a cluster of 3–12 bright pink, yellow-centered flowers. Basal leaves are oblong.

Habitat: Shaded woodlands and along waterways.

Comments: Common along trails in the foothills and mountains. Blooms June–August.

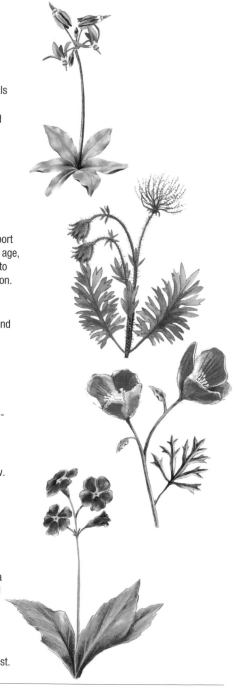

SHOWY MILKWEED
Asclepias speciosa

Size: To 4 ft. (1.2 m)

Description: Red-purplish, horned flowers bloom in tight clusters May–August. Large, fleshy leaves are finely haired. In autumn, long seed pods split open to release thousands of conspicuous, long-plumed seeds.

Habitat: Dry soils in disturbed areas and ditches, open forests.

Comments: Both the leaves and stems secrete a sticky fluid to protect the flowers from crawling insects.

FIREWEED
Chamerion angustifolium

Size: To 7 ft. (2.1 m)

Description: Distinguished by a long conical spike of bright pink, 4-petalled flowers.

Habitat: Very common in open woodlands, clearings and burned-out areas at upper elevations.

Comments: Often grows in dense colonies and tints entire fields a shade of pink. Blooms June–September.

TWINFLOWER
Linnaea borealis

Size: To 4 in. (10 cm)

Description: Trailing shrub has rounded, opposite, evergreen leaves. Slender stems support nodding pairs of pink, bell-shaped flowers.

Habitat: Moist woods.

Comments: Flowers are sweetly fragrant. Blooms May–July.

INDIAN PAINTBRUSH
Castilleja spp.

Size: To 3 ft. (90 cm)

Description: Ragged red wildflower often grows in dense colonies.

Habitat: Woodlands and mountain meadows.

Comments: Related to snapdragons, paintbrushes occur in a variety of colors. Many are often parasitic on the roots of other plants. Blooms March–October.

SPOTTED CORALROOT
Corallorhiza maculata
Size: 8–32 in. (20–80 cm)
Description: Nearly leafless plant has yellow or red-purple stems bearing loose clusters of blossoms the same color as the stems.
Habitat: Shady spruce, pine and aspen forests.
Comments: Stems often occur in clumps over extensive colonies. Blooms April–September.

ELEPHANT'S HEAD
Pedicularis groenlandica
Size: 6–30 in. (15–75 cm)
Description: Leafy stems support pink flowers resembling an elephant's head with floppy ears and a long, curling trunk.
Habitat: Wet meadows, along streamsides.
Comments: Also called little red elephants, the flower design is conducive to pollination by bees. Blooms June–August. A favorite browse for elk.

JOE-PYE WEED
Eutrochium maculatum
Size: 2–6 ft. (.6–1.8 m)
Description: Stem is stout and purple or purple-spotted. Leaves grow in whorls of 3–5. Pink to purple flowers occur in flat-topped clusters.
Habitat: Moist soils from plains to foothills.
Comments: Plant was named for a Native American medicine man – Joe Pye – who used the plant to cure many ills. Blooms July–September.

SKYROCKET
Ipomopsis aggregata
Size: 12–36 in. (30–90 cm)
Description: Bright scarlet, trumpet-shaped flowers flare at the mouth into five separate lobes and resemble exploded fireworks.
Habitat: Dry soils.
Comments: Also called desert trumpets, scarlet gilia and skunk flower, the plant has a skunky odor. Blooms May–September.

MOSS CAMPION
Silene acaulis

Size: To 2 in. (5 cm)

Description: A low-growing, mat-forming plant has pink, tubular flowers.

Habitat: Moist areas above the timberline.

Comments: The plant lacks stems and is held in place by a sturdy taproot to help it withstand frigid alpine winds. Blooms June–August.

ROCKY MOUNTAIN BEE PLANT
Cleome serrulata

Size: To 5 ft. (1.5 m)

Description: Leaves have three leaflets and occur along branching stems. Showy clusters of pinkish (sometimes white) flowers bloom June–September.

Habitat: Sandy soils, waste areas from the plains to the foothills.

Comments: Also called stinkweed for its strong odor, it is a favorite of bees. Native Americans boiled the strong leaves for food and as a stomachache remedy.

WOOD'S ROSE
Rosa woodsii

Size: 3–10 ft. (.6–3 m)

Description: Bushy shrub has widely spaced, sharply toothed leaves. Showy, fragrant 5-petalled flowers are pinkish and have yellow centers. Flowers are succeeded by hard red fruits called hips.

Habitat: Moist, rocky soils in a variety of habitats to elevations of 11,000 ft. (3300 m).

Comments: One of several similar species. Rose hip tea is an excellent source of vitamin C. Blooms May–July.

CARDINAL FLOWER
Lobelia cardinalis

Size: 1–6 ft. (.3–1.8 m)

Description: Plant with spike of striking, red tubular flowers. Flowers have three spreading lower petals and two upper petals. Lance-shaped leaves have toothed edges.

Habitat: Wet areas, along waterways, shady slopes.

Comments: Also called scarlet lobelia, it depends on hummingbirds for pollination since most insects have difficulty navigating the flowerhead. Blooms June–October.

NODDING ONION
Allium cernuum
Size: 6–20 in. (15–50 cm)
Description: Slender stalks have grass-like leaves. Pinkish flowers bloom in a nodding cluster.
Habitat: Moist soils in a variety of habitats.
Comments: Entire plant has an onion-like odor. Several similar species occur throughout the west that have edible – though often unpalatable – bulbs. Blooms June–October.

AMERICAN VETCH
Vicia americana
Size: Stems to 7 ft. (2.1 m) long.
Description: Slender climbing or sprawling plant has tubular, pea-shaped flowers that are pink-purple to red-lavender.
Habitat: Open woodlands, roadsides, waste areas.
Comments: Blooms May–July.

LEWIS' MONKEYFLOWER
Mimulus lewisii
Size: To 3 ft. (90 cm)
Description: Leafy, several-stemmed plant has showy, deep pink to red flowers with maroon blotches and dark lines in the throat.
Habitat: Wet areas in the mountains.
Comments: Striking mountain flower blooms June–August.

FAIRY SLIPPER
Calypso bulbosa
Size: To 8 in. (20 cm)
Description: Reddish flower stalk supports a stunning pink pendant flower with an inflated lower lip resembling a lady's slipper. There is a single basal leaf.
Habitat: Mossy woods.
Comments: Lives on poor soils but is capable of making its own food. Blooms March–July.

FIRECRACKER PENSTEMON
Penstemon eatonii
Size: 1–2 ft. (30–60 cm)

Description: Brilliant scarlet tubular flowers bloom in an elongate cluster. Deep green leaves grow in pairs along the stem.

Habitat: Dry, rocky slopes, fields and roadsides.

Comments: Also called Eaton's penstemon and scarlet bugler, it is a favorite of hummingbirds. Blooms May–June.

STICKY GERANIUM
Geranium viscosissimum
Size: 1–3 ft. (30–90 cm)

Description: Several-stemmed plant has long-stalked leaves and an open cluster of pink-lavender to purplish flowers.

Habitat: Open woodlands and meadows.

Comments: Leaf stems and flower stalks are sticky to the touch. Also called crane's bill. Blooms May–August.

PUSSYTOES
Antennaria spp.
Size: 4–22 in. (10–55 cm)

Description: Plant is easily distinguished by its small, fluffy, white to pinkish flowerheads that feel like the toes of a kitten. Stalks are often woolly.

Habitat: Moist soils in meadows and open woodlands from the foothills to subalpine regions.

Comments: Also called cat's paws. Blooms June–August. Leaves and stems were chewed like gum by Native Americans.

SCARLET GAURA
Gaura coccinea
Size: 6–25 in. (15–60 cm)

Description: Grayish plant has leafy stems with alternate, lance-shaped leaves. Red-pink flowers bloom in nodding clusters.

Habitat: Sandy soils in grasslands and pinyon-juniper woodlands.

Comments: Also called scarlet beeblossom. Blooms May–September.

BLUE & PURPLE FLOWERS

BLUE COLUMBINE
Aquilegia coerulea
Size: To 3 ft. (90 cm)
Description: Bushy plant has beautiful blue and white, spurred flowers tipped upwards exposing the yellow stamens.
Habitat: Mountains, aspen groves.
Comments: Popular in cultivation, several color variants exist. The law prohibits digging or uprooting this plant on public lands. Blooms June–August.

Colorado's State Flower

PURPLE LOCOWEED
Oxytropis lambertii
Size: To 16 in. (40 cm)
Description: Covered with silvery hairs, the stems support elongated clusters of pink to purplish, pea-like flowers.
Habitat: Plains and open forests.
Comments: One of several similar species of poisonous plants, this species is deadly to most livestock, causing them to go crazy ("loco" in Spanish) before they die. Blooms June–September.

SKY PILOT
Polemonium viscosum
Size: 4–16 in. (10–40 cm)
Description: Leafy plant is topped with loose clusters of funnel-shaped blue-violet flowers. The leaves are divided into leaflets that are further divided into 3–7 tiny lobes.
Habitat: Open rocky areas in the mountains.
Comments: Also called skunkweed, the stem and leaves are covered in sticky hairs and exude a skunky odor. Blooms June–August.

ROCKY MOUNTAIN FRINGED GENTIAN
Gentianopsis thermalis
Size: To 14 in. (35 cm)
Description: Blue-purple flowers have delicately fringed petals.
Habitat: Moist meadows, streambanks in mountainous regions.
Comments: Named for the thermal pools in Yellowstone National Park where it is designated the park flower. Blooms July–August.

PASQUE FLOWER
Pulsatilla patens
Size: To 15 in. (38 cm)
Description: Hairy plant has stems topped with lavender, blue or purple flowers with 5–7 petal-like sepals. Stamens are yellow.
Habitat: Prairies to mountain slopes.
Comments: Also called wild crocus, it is a harbinger of spring and often pokes through the snow. Its cousin, *Crocus sativus*, is the source of the spice saffron. Blooms March–August.

NUTTALL'S LARKSPUR
Delphinium nuttallianum
Size: 4–16 in. (10–40 cm)
Description: Showy blue flowers have 5 petal-like sepals that curve back on themselves and a prominent spur at the end. Leaves are primarily basal and have 3–7 toothed lobes.
Habitat: Sagebrush deserts, open pine woodlands.
Comments: Also called twolobe larkspur. The plant is poisonous to cattle but not to sheep.

HAREBELL
Campanula rotundifolia
Size: 4–40 in. (10–120 cm)
Description: Plant with grass-like leaves and a drooping cluster of pale blue, bell-shaped flowers. Basal leaves are rounded.
Habitat: Dry mountain meadows, rocky slopes.
Comments: Also called mountain bellflower, witches' thimble and bluebell. The name is believed to be associated with the belief that witches could transform themselves into hares. Blooms June–September.

BEEBALM
Monarda fistulosa
Size: To 4 ft. (1.2 m)
Description: Showy flowers are pink to lavender and grow in clusters of 20–50. Lance-shaped leaves are toothed.
Habitat: Dry fields, thickets, open areas.
Comments: Also called horsemint and wild bergamot, this favorite of bees is often used for teas and as a medicinal plant. Blooms June–August.

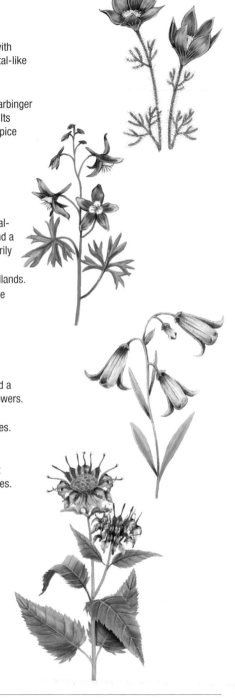

STICKY ASTER
Machaeranthera bigelovii
Size: 1–3 ft. (30–90 cm)

Description: Branching stems have sharp-toothed leaves. Showy flowers have purple to red-lavender rays surrounding a yellow central disk.

Habitat: Plains and coniferous forests.

Comments: Also called tansy aster. At night, or when the flowers are shaded, the rays fold upward. Blooms August–October.

SILKY PHACELIA
Phacelia sericea
Size: To 16 in. (40 cm)

Description: Leaves are up to 4 in. (10 cm) long and divided into many lobes. Purple, bell-shaped flowers bloom in a dense, cylindrical, terminal spike. Elongate stamens are tipped in yellow-orange pollen sacs.

Habitat: Open woodlands, roadsides, meadows, mountains.

Comments: Also called purple pincushion, alpine phacelia and purple fringe. Blooms June–August.

BLUE FLAX
Linum lewisii
Size: To 24 in. (60 cm)

Description: Unbranched leafy stems support delicate blue, 5-petalled, yellow-centered flowers.

Habitat: Well-drained soils in prairies and meadows.

Comments: Also called prairie flax, linseed oil is derived from its seeds. Native Americans used its wiry stems to make rope and fishing lines. Blooms March–September

DAYFLOWER
Commelina communis
Size: To 3 ft. (90 cm)

Description: Sprawling plant has upright stems supporting striking flowers with two large, rounded blue upper petals and a small white lower petal.

Habitat: Open woodlands, weedy areas.

Comments: Named for its short-lived blossoms. Introduced from Asia. Blooms May–October.

MONKSHOOD
Aconitum columbianum
Size: 1–6 ft. (.3–1.8 m)
Description: Leafy plant has hood-like, deep blue flowers.
Habitat: Mountain meadows, moist woods.
Comments: Also called aconite. Blooms June–September. All parts of the plant are poisonous to humans and livestock.

ROCKY MOUNTAIN IRIS
Iris missouriensis
Size: To 20 in. (50 cm)
Description: Slender stalks support large blue to violet flowers. Petals have a central yellow-orange stripe and purple veins are often visible. Narrow basal leaves are sword-shaped.
Habitat: Wet mountain habitats.
Comments: Often grows in dense clumps in meadows and along streams. Leaf fibers were once used to make rope. Blooms May–July.

BLUE-EYED GRASS
Sisyrinchium angustifolium
Size: To 2 ft. (60 cm)
Description: Slender stems support one or more delicate, 6-petalled, star-shaped, blue-violet flowers.
Habitat: Moist areas in woodlands and meadows.
Comments: Related to popular ornamentals including freesias and gladiolas. Blooms March–September.

SILVERY LUPINE
Lupinus argenteus
Size: 1–5 ft. (.3–1.5 m)
Description: Slender erect plant has star-like leaves with 5–9 leaflets. Violet, pea-like flowers bloom in an elongate terminal cluster arranged in whorls around the stem.
Habitat: Rocky soils in sagebrush flats, grasslands, open forests.
Comments: A favorite of bumblebees and butterflies, it is one of several similar species of Colorado lupines. Seeds are toxic to humans and animals. Blooms June–August.

PURPLE PRAIRIE CLOVER
Dalea purpurea
Size: 1–3 ft. (30–90 cm)
Description: Leaves typically have 5 narrow leaflets. Red-lavender flowers bloom in a long terminal spike.
Habitat: Meadows, grasslands and open coniferous forests.
Comments: Nectar and pollen attract bees, butterflies, wasps and flies. Used extensively to protect areas from erosion and for adding nitrogen to the soil. Blooms May–August.

NETTLELEAF HORSEMINT
Agastache urticifolia
Size: To 5 ft. (1.5 m)
Description: Leaves are triangular, toothed and widely spaced on 4-sided stems. Aromatic, pale pink to lavender flowers bloom in a long, terminal spike and have long stamens extending beyond the petal margin.
Habitat: Open woodlands.
Comments: Also called nettleleaf giant hyssop. Blooms June–August.

VENUS'S LOOKING GLASS
Triodanis perfoliata
Size: To 2 ft. (60 cm)
Description: Erect stems are leafy and support a few, wheel-shaped violet blue flowers that bloom in the axils of upper leaves.
Habitat: Rocky areas in woodlands and plains, disturbed soils.
Comments: Also called clasping bellflower. Blooms April–July.

ALPINE FORGET-ME-NOT
Eritrichium nanum
Size: To 4 in. (10 cm)
Description: Low-growing, cushion-like plants have hairy leaves and deep blue, yellow-centered flowers.
Habitat: Rocky soils in alpine areas.
Comments: Blooms June–August.

MOUNTAIN BLUEBELL
Mertensia ciliata
Size: 10–60 in. (25–150 cm)
Description: Leafy stems support loose clusters of bell-shaped blue flowers that turn pinkish with age.
Habitat: Streambanks and wet areas.
Comments: Also called streamside bluebells and tall fringed bluebells. Blooms May–August.

PRAIRIE SPIDERWORT
Tradescantia occidentalis
Size: 8–20 in. (20–50 cm)
Description: Slender plant has long, narrow leaves. Delicate, papery, blue flowers have yellow anthers.
Habitat: Plains, grasslands, open woodlands.
Comments: Also called the western spiderwort. Native Americans used the cooked plant as a vegetable. Blooms July–September.

WILD MINT
Mentha arvensis
Size: 8–32 in. (20–80 cm)
Description: Opposite leaves are broadly lanceolate and sharply toothed. Lavender to pink flowers bloom in dense clusters at the leaf axils.
Habitat: Moist areas, along streams.
Comments: Entire plant smells strongly of mint. Blooms July–September.

CHICORY
Cichorium intybus
Size: 1–6 ft. (.3–1.8 m)
Description: Wiry branching plant has wheel-shaped flowers in varying shades of blue that are toothed on their outer edge.
Habitat: Roadsides, fields, waste areas.
Comments: Introduced from Eurasia, it is grown for its root, which can be dried, roasted and ground to make a coffee substitute. Blooms March–October. Its relative endive (*C. endivia*) is cultivated as a salad plant.

COLORADO ECOREGIONS

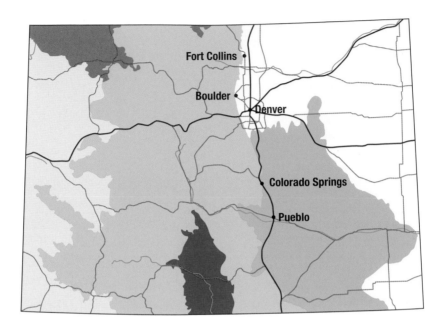

Colorado Plateau
Southern Rockies
Arizona/New Mexico Plateau
High Plains
Southwestern Tablelands
Wyoming Basin

COLORADO TOURISM REGIONS

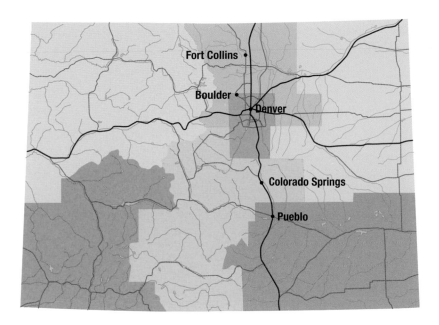

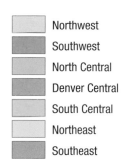

	Northwest
	Southwest
	North Central
	Denver Central
	South Central
	Northeast
	Southeast

NORTHWEST

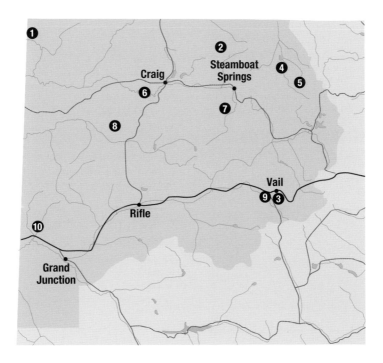

1 - BROWNS PARK NATIONAL WILDLIFE REFUGE

Browns Park National Wildlife Refuge (NWR) was established in 1963 to provide habitat for migratory birds. The Green River runs through the heart of the 13,455-acre Refuge, providing the life blood for the wetlands and cottonwood forests. The threatened Ute's ladies' tresses orchid and hundreds of species of animals depend on the habitat that the Refuge provides.

2 - STEAMBOAT LAKE STATE PARK

Steamboat Lake State Park features a 1,100 surface-acre reservoir located at 8,000 feet in elevation in the Willow Creek Valley of the Park Range. There is plenty of geology, plants and wildlife to explore in this beautiful setting. Routt National Forest helps to preserve large tracts of contiguous habitat in the region. Over 200 species of migratory and resident birds are seen in the park.

3 - VAIL NATURE CENTER

This seven-acre facility, in the heart of Vail, is a tranquil gem to explore the web of trails along Gore Creek or learn from the exhibits about the local native species of plants and animals.

4 - ARAPAHO NATIONAL WILDLIFE REFUGE

The refuge was established in 1967 to provide waterfowl with a suitable place to nest and rear their young. It was created in part to offset losses of nesting habitat in the prairie wetland region of the Midwest.

5 - STATE FOREST STATE PARK

State Forest State Park in Walden offers an idyllic destination to escape crowds in Rocky Mountain National Park and is one of the best spots to view moose in the state. It also boasts some of the most spectacular scenery around, including glistening alpine lakes and dramatic mountain peaks.

6 - YAMPA RIVER CORRIDOR AND YAMPA RIVER STATE WILDLIFE AREA

The headquarters on the Yampa River near Hayden, Colorado, provides excellent camping, a Visitor Center and nature trail. A 134-mile stretch of the Yampa River is the heart of Yampa River State Park. The Elkhead Reservoir is the third major component of the Yampa River State Park system. Visitors can enjoy swimming, boating, fishing, camping and picnicking at the lake.

7 - STAGECOACH STATE PARK AND WETLAND HABITAT PRESERVE

Stagecoach State Park features a 780-surface-acre reservoir lying in the Yampa River Valley of the northern Rocky Mountains. Over 200 species of migratory and resident birds are recorded for this area.

8 - RIO BLANCO LAKE STATE WILDLIFE AREA

The best lake in the area for waterbirds, shorebirds and trophy pike. While driving to or from the lake, keep watch for bald eagles and sandhill cranes, especially during the spring and fall.

9 - BETTY FORD ALPINE GARDENS

Betty Ford Alpine Gardens is an internationally acclaimed botanic garden known for its alpine horticulture, education and conservation. Located in the small resort town of Vail, Colorado, it is the highest elevation botanical garden in the world situated at 8,200 ft. (2700 m).

10 - HIGHLINE LAKE STATE PARK

The National Audubon Society has named Highline Lake an Important Bird Area with more than 200 species found here. Many migratory and resident birds including waterfowl, shorebirds, neotropical songbirds and raptors are attracted to the reservoir and adjacent uplands.

SOUTHWEST

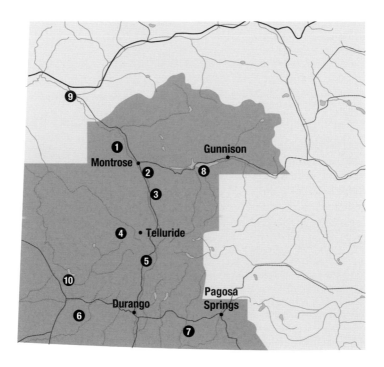

1 - ESCALANTE WILDLIFE AREA

The highlight at this large state wildlife area is a good-sized pond, where you can see a variety of ducks, shorebirds when the water levels are right and sandhill cranes. Designated as an Audubon Important Bird Area.

2 - MONTROSE BOTANIC GARDENS

Located in the high desert community of Montrose, Colorado, the Montrose Botanic Gardens are an inspiration and an invaluable educational site for residents as they strive to enhance a landscape that was once tumbleweed, sage and cactus.

3 - SOUTHWEST RIDGWAY STATE PARK

If variety is what you're looking for, Ridgway's got it. Watch for different species of waterfowl and shorebirds such as American avocets and western grebes. Winter species include nuthatches and great horned owls; in the summer you might see American dippers, mountain bluebirds and red-tailed hawks.

4 - WOODS LAKE STATE WILDLIFE AREA

This is a small, beautiful and secluded lake set among mixed-conifer forest and aspen groves. The mountain scenery here is spectacular, with beautiful views of Mount Wilson. Rugged trails lead into the Lizard Head Wilderness Area and, eventually, to alpine tundra.

5 - SAN JUAN SKYWAY

Traveling through the magnificent San Juan Mountains in southwestern Colorado is one of the most unforgettable experiences, with some of the country's most jaw-dropping scenery, multiple historic towns and sites and lots of wildlife. It traverses through Durango, Silverton, Telluride and Ouray on a 236-mile route that was named by *Travel + Leisure* as one of the best drives in the nation.

6 - MESA VERDE NATIONAL PARK

Mesa Verde contains several habitats that support a great diversity of resident and migratory wildlife. The park has been named a Colorado Important Bird Area (IBA) by the Audubon Society. The Nature Conservancy has classified all of Mesa Verde National Park within their Network of Conservation Areas (NCA) because of exceptional occurrences of rare plant and animal species.

7 - CHIMNEY ROCK NATIONAL MONUMENT

This off-the-beaten-path archaeological site is located at the southern edge of the San Juan Mountains in southwestern Colorado. Attractions include 200 ancient homes and ceremonial buildings and abundant wildlife set in the breathtaking San Juan National Forest.

8 - BLACK CANYON OF THE GUNNISON NATIONAL MONUMENT

Big enough to be overwhelming, still intimate enough to feel the pulse of time, Black Canyon of the Gunnison exposes you to some of the steepest cliffs, oldest rock and craggiest spires in North America. With two million years to work, the Gunnison River, along with the forces of weathering, has sculpted this vertical wilderness of rock, water and sky.

9 - COLORADO NATIONAL MONUMENT

Towering monoliths exist within a vast plateau and canyon panorama. You can experience sheer-walled red rock canyons along the twists and turns of Rim Rock Drive, where you may spy bighorn sheep and soaring eagles.

10 - MCPHEE RESERVOIR

One of the largest reservoirs in the state, McPhee Reservoir features pinyon pine and Douglas fir woodlands that support a diversity of wildlife including deer, elk, bobcats, owls, eagles and osprey.

NORTH CENTRAL

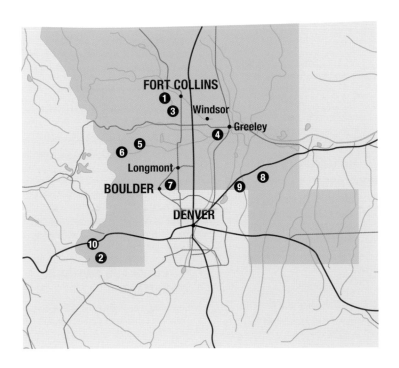

1 - LORY STATE PARK

From rolling valleys to mountainous hillsides, Lory State Park's variety of trails are great for short or long hikes, mountain bike rides, horseback rides and trail runs. Backcountry camping is also available. Visitor center.

2 - ARAPAHO-ROOSEVELT NATIONAL FOREST & PAWNEE NATIONAL GRASSLAND

Known collectively as ARP, these public lands flank the Rocky Mountains and the foothills on both sides of the Continental Divide. Activities include, hiking, camping, wildlife viewing, horseback riding, fishing, hunting and skiing. Keep your eyes peeled for abundant raptors and pronghorns.

3 - CATHY FROMME PRAIRIE NATURAL AREA

Cathy Fromme Prairie is a rare example of pre-settlement shortgrass prairie landscape. Drylands and wetlands here provide habitat to a variety of plants and animals.

4 - BIG THOMPSON CANYON

Big Thompson Canyon is an extraordinary drive from Loveland to Estes Park. As one of Colorado's most eminent scenic excursions, you'll see the Big Thompson River and paramount rock formations.

5 - ESTES VALLEY AND ESTES PARK

As the gateway to Rocky Mountain National Park, Estes Park is a tourist destination with a scenic river walk, hiking and picnicking on Lake Estes and a 4.5-acre bird sanctuary.

6 - ROCKY MOUNTAIN NATIONAL PARK

The Northern Front Range, including the Peak to Peak Scenic and Historic Byway, is the gateway to some of Colorado's best wildlife viewing prospects. It is the natural habitat of more than 900 species of Colorado wildlife. A drive up Trail Ridge Road takes you through several ecosystems with spectacular vistas.

7 - WALDEN PONDS WILDLIFE HABITAT AND SAWHILL PONDS

Wetland habitats nestled within the surrounding Great Plains support aquatic plant and animal life and attract large numbers of migrating bird species.

8 - THE WILD ANIMAL SANCTUARY

Over 300 animals living in open habitats are free to roam. The sanctuary specializes in rescuing and caring for large predators that have been ill-treated, for which their owners can no longer care, or which might otherwise be euthanized.

9 - BARR LAKE STATE PARK

One of the top birding areas in the state, Barr Lake is home to more than 370 species of resident and migratory birds. In the summer, white pelicans, cormorants and egrets join the pairs of nesting great blue herons and bald eagles. Barr Lake is also the headquarters of the Rocky Mountain Bird Observatory.

10 - GRAYS AND TORREY PEAKS

Wildlife in the area includes mountain goat, pika, cougar or mountain lion, mule deer, elk, marmot, coyote, ptarmigan, American red squirrel and gray jay or Canada jay.

DENVER CENTRAL

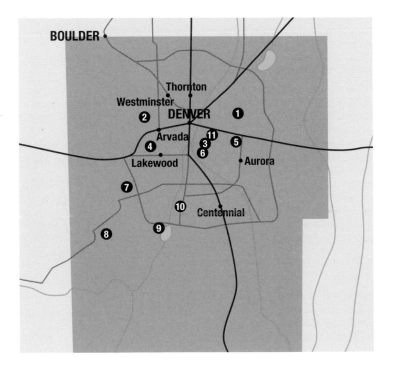

1 - ROCKY MOUNTAIN ARSENAL NATIONAL WILDLIFE REFUGE

15,000 acres of land just 10 miles outside of Denver in Commerce City harbors over 280 native plants and 330 animal species, including mule deer, coyotes, bison, prairie dogs, songbirds, burrowing owls and bald eagles. It is now one of the largest refuges in the country.

2 - TWO PONDS NATIONAL WILDLIFE REFUGE

Two Ponds National Wildlife Refuge serves as an oasis for wildlife and people throughout the Denver Metro area. It covers 63 acres of uplands, 9 acres of wetlands and 3 small ponds that contain various species of native flora and fauna.

3 - DENVER MUSEUM OF NATURE & SCIENCE

Founder Edwin Carter assembled one of the most complete collections of Colorado fauna then in existence. Today, it is one of the premier museums in the western United States teaching natural history and includes an Imax theater and planetarium shows.

4 - CROWN HILL PARK AND WILDLIFE PRESERVE

A natural haven amid a suburban neighborhood, Crown Hill park is a place to retreat, admire abundant birdlife and enjoy lake-side recreation.

5 - BLUFF LAKE NATURE CENTER

The refuge is home to an abundance of animals and native plants that thrive in a variety of habitats. Bluff Lake is Denver's largest open space managed as native habitat and Denver's only nonprofit nature center.

6 - DENVER BOTANIC GARDENS

Denver Botanic Gardens strives to entertain and delight while educating through outreach and visitor's collaboration. The Plains Garden, the Gates Garden and the Rock Alpine Garden all highlight native species.

7 - MORRISON NATURAL HISTORY MUSEUM

Discover Colorado's dinosaurs with expert guides and hands-on exhibits at Jefferson County's original paleontology museum. The Morrison Natural History Museum has been featured in Smithsonian magazine and media outlets around the world.

8 - MOUNT EVANS SCENIC BYWAY

This is the highest paved road in North America, reaching over 14,000 feet. The views from the top and on the way up – above the tree line – are outstanding, with a good chance of seeing wildlife, particularly bighorn sheep. (Closed in winter).

9 - CHATFIELD STATE PARK/ ROCKY MOUNTAIN BIRD OBSERVATORY

Chatfield State Park is home to more than 300 species of birds at some times of the year. A banding station, viewing blinds and heron rookery all contribute to making this one of Colorado's best birding spots.

10 - SOUTH PLATTE PARK AND CARSON NATURE CENTER

878 acres of open space offers 5 lakes open to fishing, 4+ miles of walking trails, a paved regional recreation trail, 2.5 miles of river, over 300 species of wildlife and a free nature center with interactive exhibits.

11 - DENVER ZOO

80-acre zoological garden located in City Park of Denver features 3,500 animals from Colorado and the rest of the world and is open every day of the year. It is the most popular paid attraction in the Denver metropolitan area.

SOUTH CENTRAL

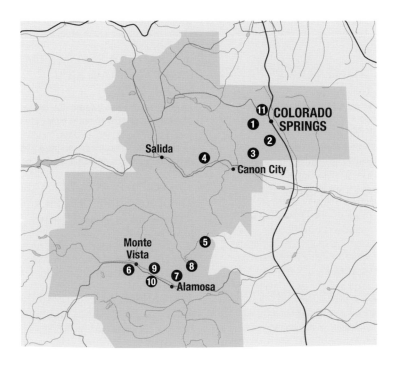

1 - BEAR CREEK REGIONAL PARK & NATURE CENTER

Interpretive programs, special events, guided and self-guided tours and media presentations are offered all year. Outside, two miles of self-guiding nature trails wind through the shortgrass prairie, scrub oak woodlands and cottonwood riparian communities.

2 - MAY NATURAL HISTORY MUSEUM

Features over 7,000 species of butterflies, moths, bizarre beetles, giant spiders, deadly scorpions and more!

3 - BEAVER CREEK STATE WILDLIFE AREA

Sanctuary encompasses habitats ranging from desert to conifer forests and meadows. Vegetation includes Douglas fir, ponderosa pine, limber pine, aspen, pinyon-juniper woodlands and wetlands streams.

4 -BIGHORN SHEEP CANYON

As the name implies, bighorn sheep populate this area. Look for them along the banks of the river and rugged mountainsides. Watch also for deer and raptors, particularly bald eagles in winter. Rafting trips are a popular way to view the area.

5 - GREAT SAND DUNES NATIONAL PARK AND PRESERVE

The park and preserve contain the tallest sand dunes in North America and ecosystems ranging from dunes and wetlands to forest to tundra – each supporting specially adapted plant, animal and insect life.

6 - RIO GRANDE STATE WILDLIFE AREA

The property is one of the few remaining large, intact tracts of private land within the Rio Grande Natural Area. The trees and brush along the river support many birds in the breeding season and many more during migration.

7 - BLANCA WILDLIFE HABITAT AREA

Flocks of shorebirds such as gulls, pelicans and sandpipers find refuge at the Blanca Wetlands along with more than 150 other bird species. Wheelchair accessible trails help to make this bird watcher's paradise accessible to all.

8 - SAN LUIS LAKES STATE PARK AND WILDLIFE AREA

San Luis State Wildlife Area (SWA) features an 890-surface-acre playa lake with water levels stabilized as in a reservoir, amid rolling sandhills and alkaline flats of San Luis Valley. The protected lands of the 2,054-acre wildlife area preserve critically-important habitat for unusual flora and fauna.

9 - RUSSELL LAKES STATE WILDLIFE AREA

A spring creek flows through this property, feeding a maze of wetlands, dikes, canals and shallow lakes designed and built to restore habitat for nesting waterfowl. Much of the site is closed February to July for nesting, but a boardwalk is open year-round.

10 - MONTE VISTA NATIONAL WILDLIFE REFUGE

Monte Vista National Wildlife Refuge is in the San Luis Valley, a high mountain basin located in south-central Colorado. It's one of three national wildlife refuges in the valley that provide crucial feeding, resting and breeding habitat for over 200 bird species and other wildlife. Thousands of sandhill cranes and few endangered whooping cranes migrate through the refuge in spring.

11 - GARDEN OF THE GODS

Garden of the Gods Park is a registered National Natural Landmark. 300 ft. of towering sandstone rock formations are framed against a backdrop of snow-capped Pikes Peak and brilliant blue skies. This world-class Visitor & Nature Center and museum is the most visited attraction in the region.

NORTHEAST

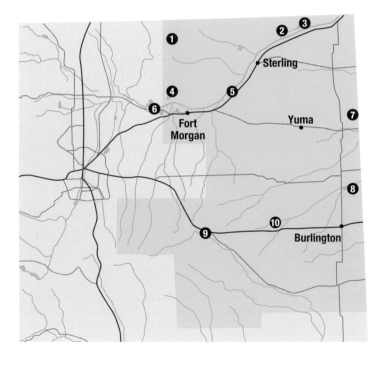

1 - PAWNEE BUTTES

The Pawnee Buttes are among the grasslands' most prominent topographic features, rising nearly 300 ft. from the high plains floor. A short trail leads down a major escarpment into a sea of open space and to the base of each butte.

2 - TAMARACK RANCH STATE WILDLIFE AREA

This site encompasses nearly 20 miles of the South Platte River and a variety of habitats including wooded bottomlands, farmed plots and sagebrush sandhills.

3 - RED LION STATE WILDLIFE AREA

Adjacent to Jumbo Reservoir, Red Lion SWA is centered around a lake affectionately known as "Little Jumbo". While not usually as productive as the larger Jumbo, the reservoir here is often filled with snow and ross's geese during winter and a few greater white-fronted geese can often also be found.

4 - JACKSON LAKE STATE PARK

Nature and wildlife abound at this oasis. Birders flock here because of the park's position in the "central fly zone" for migratory birds. Anglers can catch any number of species. Wildlife watchers or photographers find the best time to observe is in winter when all is quiet.

5 - PREWITT RESERVOIR STATE WILDLIFE AREA

Prewitt Reservoir is nestled in a vibrant ecosystem in northeast Colorado. The lake is around 2,400 acres when full and offers year-round recreation. The area is full of wildlife, especially waterfowl. The reservoir is also calmer and less windy than nearby North Sterling Res or Jackson Lake. Nature viewing and birding is phenomenal in the park, with a unique prairieland setting.

6 - SOUTH PLATTE RIVER EAGLE DRIVING TOUR

More than 100 bald eagles can be seen perched in the cottonwood trees along the South Platte River Trail that follows Highway 34 between Fort Morgan and Kersey. The best time to view the roosting eagles is in the early morning hours or an hour or so before dusk.

7 - GREATER PRAIRIE-CHICKEN LEKS

Leks, or dancing grounds, are flat, open grassland areas used by successive generations of prairie-chickens during spring courtship. The sand sage prairie just north of Wray contains the vast majority of Colorado's greater prairie-chickens. The only reliable lek locations at this time are located on private lands. Several groups and ranches operate tours to see the chickens on their leks in spring.

8 - SOUTH REPUBLICAN STATE WILDLIFE AREA

This location covers most of the area below the dam at Bonny. Habitat varies from yucca grassland and large hedgerows to lowland riparian. The hedgerow at Hale is enormous and a good spot for northern cardinals, sparrows during the winter, owls and migrants.

9 - LIMON WETLANDS

The Limon Wetlands provide a habitat for wildlife. Migrating birds use the plentiful food sources of wetlands as "refueling stations" on their long flights every spring and fall. In the summer many birds build their nests amid the dense wetland plants.

10 - FLAGLER RESERVOIR STATE WILDLIFE AREA

Because this is one of the only reservoirs in the area, the water and large trees here act as an excellent migrant trap. The grassland to the east is of fairly high quality. Look also for deer, pronghorn, rattlesnakes and the regal fritillary (a magnificent and rare butterfly).

SOUTHEAST

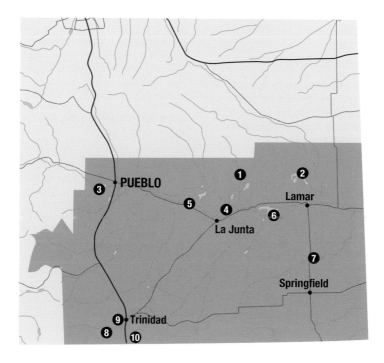

1 - ADOBE CREEK RESERVOIR STATE WILDLIFE AREA

The site consists of a lake with an island (known as Tern Island), surrounded by shortgrass prairie. In most years, Tern Island is the primary least tern nesting site in the state of Colorado. The site serves as a significant migration and staging location for thousands of shorebirds, hundreds of gulls and up to 100 black and forsters terns.

2 - QUEENS STATE WILDLIFE AREA

This state wildlife area encompasses several large open reservoirs: Neenoshe, Neegronda, Neesopah and Upper and Lower Queens – surrounded by agricultural fields and shortgrass prairie.

3 - PUEBLO ZOO

Home to more than 500 animals representing 125 different species from around the world.

4 - BENT'S OLD FORT NATIONAL HISTORIC SITE AND BENT'S BIRD SANCTUARY

Bent's Old Fort National Historic Site near La Junta has recorded over 135 species of birds. Many of the birds visit the marshy wetlands near the fort and others are known to nest on the grasslands nearby. Bent's Bird Sanctuary located behind the Bent's Fort Inn near Las Animas is an ideal setting for bird watching. There are five trails and feeding stations, taking you along the waterways and under the shade trees.

5 - ROCKY FORD STATE WILDLIFE AREA

Excellent riparian habitat and thickets support large populations of sparrows, owls, squirrels, muskrat and deer. The sewage ponds just northeast of Rocky Ford can be great for shorebirds and waterbirds, depending on water levels.

6 - JOHN MARTIN RESERVOIR STATE PARK

This premier birding area has nearly 400 documented species of birds. Two federally protected shorebirds, the least tern and the piping plover, nest here in spring and summer.

7 - TWO BUTTES RESERVOIR AND STATE WILDLIFE AREA

Below the dam habitats include extensive tangles of underbrush, tall trees, marshy ponds and grassy areas. This area can be excellent any time of year, but especially during migration; it is probably the best public area in Colorado to find roadrunners.

8 - TRINIDAD LAKE STATE PARK/ LONGS CANYON WATCHABLE WILDLIFE AREA

Miles of trails winding through ancient and interesting local history and spectacular scenery provide visitors and nature enthusiasts with great outdoor exploration opportunities. The mild climate and large lake are ideal for water sports.

9 - LOUDEN-HENRITZE ARCHAEOLOGY MUSEUM

The museum houses all kinds of treasures including dinosaur bones, pottery, models of ancient village life and burials and even a fish that lived on the Santa Fe Trail when Trinidad was a seabed.

10 - JAMES M. JOHN & LAKE DOROTHEY STATE WILDLIFE AREAS

These remote SWAs are the only two SWAs in Colorado that you must leave the state to access via road. Habitats include ponderosa forest, mixed conifer woodland and oak scrub that support a variety of birds and large mammals including black bear, mule deer, elk and mountain lion.

MAMMALS
- [ ] Abert's Squirrel
- [ ] American Badger
- [ ] American Beaver
- [ ] American Bison
- [ ] American Pika
- [ ] Bighorn Sheep
- [ ] Black Bear
- [ ] Black-tailed Jackrabbit
- [ ] Black-tailed Prairie Dog
- [ ] Bobcat
- [ ] Brazilian Free-tailed Bat
- [ ] Bushy-tailed Woodrat
- [ ] Colorado Chipmunk
- [ ] Common Gray Fox
- [ ] Common Muskrat
- [ ] Common Porcupine
- [ ] Common Raccoon
- [ ] Coyote
- [ ] Deer Mouse
- [ ] Desert Cottontail
- [ ] Elk
- [ ] Golden-mantled Ground Squirrel
- [ ] House Mouse
- [ ] Little Brown Bat
- [ ] Long-tailed Weasel
- [ ] Masked Shrew
- [ ] Mink
- [ ] Moose
- [ ] Mountain Cottontail
- [ ] Mountain Goat
- [ ] Mountain Lion
- [ ] Mule Deer
- [ ] Northern Pocket Gopher
- [ ] Northern River Otter
- [ ] Norway Rat
- [ ] Ord's Kangaroo Rat
- [ ] Pronghorn
- [ ] Red Fox
- [ ] Red Squirrel
- [ ] Ringtail
- [ ] Rock Squirrel
- [ ] Short-tailed Weasel
- [ ] Snowshoe Hare
- [ ] Southern Red-backed Vole
- [ ] Striped Skunk
- [ ] Thirteen-lined Ground Squirrel
- [ ] Townsend's Big-eared Bat
- [ ] Virginia Opossum
- [ ] Western Jumping Mouse
- [ ] Western Spotted Skunk
- [ ] White-tailed Antelope Squirrel
- [ ] White-tailed Deer
- [ ] White-tailed Jackrabbit
- [ ] Wyoming Ground Squirrel
- [ ] Yellow-bellied Marmot

BIRDS
- [ ] American Avocet
- [ ] American Coot
- [ ] American Crow
- [ ] American Dipper
- [ ] American Goldfinch
- [ ] American Kestrel
- [ ] American Robin
- [ ] American White Pelican
- [ ] American Wigeon
- [ ] Bald Eagle
- [ ] Barn Swallow
- [ ] Belted Kingfisher
- [ ] Black-billed Magpie
- [ ] Black-capped Chickadee
- [ ] Black-chinned Hummingbird
- [ ] Black-crowned Night-heron
- [ ] Black-necked Stilt
- [ ] Blue Jay
- [ ] Blue-winged Teal
- [ ] Brewer's Blackbird
- [ ] Broad-tailed Hummingbird
- [ ] Brown Creeper
- [ ] Brown-headed Cowbird
- [ ] Bufflehead
- [ ] Bullock's Oriole
- [ ] Burrowing Owl
- [ ] Bushtit
- [ ] California Gull
- [ ] Canada Goose
- [ ] Canada Jay
- [ ] Cedar Waxwing
- [ ] Chipping Sparrow
- [ ] Cinnamon Teal
- [ ] Cliff Swallow
- [ ] Common Goldeneye
- [ ] Common Grackle
- [ ] Common Merganser

☐ Common Raven
☐ Cooper's Hawk
☐ Dark-eyed Junco
☐ Double-crested Cormorant
☐ Downy Woodpecker
☐ Dusky Grouse
☐ European Starling
☐ Evening Grosbeak
☐ Ferruginous Hawk
☐ Gadwall
☐ Gambel's Quail
☐ Golden Eagle
☐ Great Blue Heron
☐ Great Egret
☐ Great Horned Owl
☐ Great-tailed Grackle
☐ Greater Prairie Chicken
☐ Greater Sage-grouse
☐ Green-winged Teal
☐ Hairy Woodpecker
☐ Herring Gull
☐ Horned Lark
☐ House Finch
☐ House Sparrow
☐ House Wren
☐ Juniper Titmouse
☐ Killdeer
☐ Lark Bunting
☐ Lewis' Woodpecker
☐ Loggerhead Shrike
☐ Mallard
☐ Mountain Bluebird
☐ Mountain Chickadee
☐ Mourning Dove
☐ Northern Flicker
☐ Northern Harrier
☐ Northern Pintail
☐ Northern Shoveler
☐ Osprey
☐ Pied-billed Grebe
☐ Pine Siskin
☐ Pinyon Jay
☐ Prairie Falcon
☐ Red Crossbill
☐ Red-breasted Nuthatch
☐ Red-tailed Hawk
☐ Red-winged Blackbird

☐ Redhead
☐ Ring-billed Gull
☐ Ring-necked Duck
☐ Ring-necked Pheasant
☐ Rock Pigeon
☐ Ruby-crowned Kinglet
☐ Ruddy Duck
☐ Sandhill Crane
☐ Say's Phoebe
☐ Sharp-shinned Hawk
☐ Snowy Egret
☐ Song Sparrow
☐ Spotted Sandpiper
☐ Spotted Towhee
☐ Steller's Jay
☐ Swainson's Hawk
☐ Townsend's Solitaire
☐ Tree Swallow
☐ Turkey Vulture
☐ Violet-green Swallow
☐ Western Bluebird
☐ Western Grebe
☐ Western Kingbird
☐ Western Meadowlark
☐ Western Tanager
☐ Western Wood-pewee
☐ White-faced Ibis
☐ White-tailed Ptarmigan
☐ White-breasted Nuthatch
☐ White-crowned Sparrow
☐ Wild Turkey
☐ Wilson's Snipe
☐ Wood Duck
☐ Woodhouse's Scrub Jay
☐ Yellow Warbler
☐ Yellow-headed Blackbird
☐ Yellow-rumped Warbler

REPTILES

☐ Bullsnake
☐ Central Plains Milk Snake
☐ Collared Lizard
☐ Fence Lizard
☐ Great Plains Rat Snake
☐ Great Plains Skink
☐ Greater Short-horned Lizard
☐ Ornate Box Turtle

- ☐ Plains Garter Snake
- ☐ Plains Hognose Snake
- ☐ Six-lined Racerunner
- ☐ Snapping Turtle
- ☐ Western Painted Turtle
- ☐ Western Rattlesnake
- ☐ Yellow-belled Racer

AMPHIBIANS

- ☐ Barred Tiger Salamander
- ☐ Bullfrog
- ☐ Chorus Frog
- ☐ Northern Leopard Frog
- ☐ Plains Spadefoot Toad
- ☐ Western Toad
- ☐ Woodhouse's Toad

FISHES

- ☐ Arctic Char
- ☐ Black Crappie
- ☐ Bluegill
- ☐ Bonytail Chub
- ☐ Brook Trout
- ☐ Brown Trout
- ☐ Channel Catfish
- ☐ Colorado Pikeminnow
- ☐ Cutthroat (Native) Trout
- ☐ Grayling
- ☐ Green Sunfish
- ☐ Humpback Chub
- ☐ Kokanee Salmon
- ☐ Lake Trout
- ☐ Largemouth Bass
- ☐ Mountain Whitefish
- ☐ Northern Pike
- ☐ Rainbow Trout
- ☐ Razorback Sucker
- ☐ Redear Sunfish
- ☐ Sauger
- ☐ Saugeye
- ☐ Smallmouth Bass
- ☐ Splake
- ☐ Tiger Muskie
- ☐ Walleye
- ☐ White Crappie
- ☐ Wiper
- ☐ Yellow Perch

BUTTERFLIES & MOTHS

- ☐ Acrea Moth
- ☐ American Tent Caterpillar Moth
- ☐ Anise Swallowtail
- ☐ Aphrodite Fritillary
- ☐ Black Swallowtail
- ☐ Banded Woollybear
- ☐ Buckeye
- ☐ Cabbage White
- ☐ Colorado Hairstreak
- ☐ Common Alpine
- ☐ Common Checkered Skipper
- ☐ Common Sulphur
- ☐ Common Wood Nymph
- ☐ Edward's Fritillary
- ☐ Fall Webworm Moth
- ☐ Five-spotted Hawkmoth
- ☐ Gorgone Checkerspot
- ☐ Gray Hairstreak
- ☐ Hackberry Emperor
- ☐ Hoary Comma
- ☐ Hummingbird Clearwing
- ☐ Imperial Moth
- ☐ Io Moth
- ☐ Melissa Blue
- ☐ Milbert's Tortoiseshell
- ☐ Miller Moth
- ☐ Monarch
- ☐ Mourning Cloak
- ☐ Northern Crescent
- ☐ Orange Sulphur
- ☐ Painted Lady
- ☐ Pale Tiger Swallowtail
- ☐ Phoebus Parnassian
- ☐ Polyphemus Moth
- ☐ Purplish Copper
- ☐ Red Admiral
- ☐ Sara Orangetip
- ☐ Satyr Comma
- ☐ Silver-spotted Skipper
- ☐ Spring Azure
- ☐ Tailed Blue
- ☐ Two-tailed Swallowtail
- ☐ Variegated Fritillary
- ☐ Viceroy
- ☐ Weidemeyer's Admiral

☐ Western Sheepmoth
☐ Western Tiger Swallowtail
☐ White-lined Sphinx

CATERPILLARS

☐ Anise Swallowtail
☐ Banded Woollybear
☐ Black Swallowtail
☐ Buckeye
☐ Cabbage White
☐ Five-spotted Hawkmoth
☐ Imperial Moth
☐ Io Moth
☐ Monarch
☐ Mourning Cloak
☐ Painted Lady
☐ Red Admiral
☐ Skipper
☐ Sulphur
☐ Tailed Blue
☐ Tent Caterpillar
☐ Tiger Swallowtail
☐ Viceroy
☐ Webworm Caterpillar
☐ White-lined Sphinx

TREES & SHRUBS

☐ Alderleaf Mountain Mahogany
☐ Big Sagebrush
☐ Bitterbrush
☐ Boxelder
☐ Broom Snakeweed
☐ Colorado Blue Spruce
☐ Colorado Pinyon Pine
☐ Common Chokecherry
☐ Douglas-fir
☐ Englemann Spruce
☐ Gambel Oak
☐ Greasewood
☐ Greenleaf Manzanita
☐ Kinnikinnick
☐ Limber Pine
☐ Lodgepole Pine
☐ Mountain Alder
☐ Mountain Currant
☐ Narrowleaf Cottonwood
☐ Peachleaf Willow

☐ Plains Cottonwood
☐ Ponderosa Pine
☐ Poison Ivy
☐ Rabbitbrush
☐ Red-osier Dogwood
☐ Rocky Mountain Bristlecone Pine
☐ Rocky Mountain Juniper
☐ Rocky Mountain Maple
☐ Serviceberry
☐ Shrubby Cinquefoil
☐ Smooth Sumac
☐ Snowberry
☐ Subalpine Fir
☐ Trembling Aspen
☐ Wax Currant
☐ White Fir

CACTI

☐ Blue Yucca
☐ Claret Cup Cactus
☐ Green Pitaya
☐ Prickly Pear Cactus
☐ Soapweed Yucca
☐ Tree Cholla

WILDFLOWERS

☐ Alpine Forget-me-not
☐ Alpine Primrose
☐ Alpine Sunflower
☐ American Globeflower
☐ American Vetch
☐ Arrowleaf Balsamroot
☐ Arrowleaf Groundsel
☐ Beebalm
☐ Black-eyed Susan
☐ Blanketflower
☐ Blue Columbine
☐ Blue Flax
☐ Blue-eyed Grass
☐ Buffalo Gourd
☐ Canada Violet
☐ Cardinal Flower
☐ Chicory
☐ Cow Parsnip
☐ Cowboy's Delight
☐ Crested Pricklepoppy
☐ Dayflower

☐ Death Camas
☐ Elephant's Head
☐ Evening Primrose
☐ Fairy Slipper
☐ Field Bindweed
☐ Firecracker Penstemon
☐ Fireweed
☐ Glacier Lily
☐ Golden Banner
☐ Goldenrod
☐ Harebell
☐ Heartleaf Arnica
☐ Indian Blanket
☐ Indian Paintbrush
☐ Joe-Pye Weed
☐ Lewis' Monkeyflower
☐ Marsh Marigold
☐ Monkshood
☐ Moss Campion
☐ Mountain Bluebell
☐ Netteleaf Horsemint
☐ Nodding Onion
☐ Nuttall's Larspur
☐ Old Man's Whiskers
☐ Oregon Grape
☐ Oxeye Daisy
☐ Parry's Lousewort
☐ Pasque Flower
☐ Pearly Everlasting
☐ Phlox
☐ Prairie Spiderwort
☐ Purple Locoweed
☐ Purple Prairie Clover
☐ Pussytoes
☐ Queen Anne's Lace
☐ Red Baneberry
☐ Rocky Mountain Bee Plant
☐ Rocky Mountain Fringed Gentian

☐ Rocky Mountain Iris
☐ Scarlet Gaura
☐ Sego Lily
☐ Shooting Star
☐ Showy Milkweed
☐ Silky Phacelia
☐ Silvery Lupine
☐ Single Delight
☐ Sky Pilot
☐ Skyrocket
☐ Snowball Saxifrage
☐ Spotted Coralroot
☐ Star-flowered Lily-of-the-valley
☐ Stemless Daisy
☐ Sticky Aster
☐ Sticky Geranium
☐ Subalpine Buttercup
☐ Sulphurflower Buckwheat
☐ Sunflower
☐ Twinflower
☐ Venus's Looking Glass
☐ Western Bistort
☐ Western Spring Beauty
☐ Western Wallflower
☐ White Mountain Avens
☐ White Trillium
☐ White Virgin's Bower
☐ Wild Candytuft
☐ Wild Mint
☐ Woolly Mullein
☐ Wood's Rose
☐ Yarrow
☐ Yellow Coneflower
☐ Yellow Monkeyflower
☐ Yellow Mountain Dandelion
☐ Yellow Salsify
☐ Yellow Stonecrop

Alternate
Spaced singly along the stem.

Anther
The part of the stamen that produces pollen.

Anadromous
Living in saltwater, breeding in freshwater.

Annual
A plant that completes its life cycle in one year.

Anterior
Pertaining to the front end.

Aquatic
Living in water.

Aquifer
Underground chamber or layer of rock that holds water.

Ascending
Rising or curving upward.

Barbel
An organ near the mouth of fish used to taste, touch or smell.

Berry
A fruit formed from a single ovary that is fleshy or pulpy and contains one or many seeds.

Bloom
A whitish powdery or waxy covering.

Brackish
Water that is part freshwater and part saltwater.

Bract
A modified, often scale-like, leaf, usually small.

Branchlet
A twig from which leaves grow.

Boss
A rounded knob between the eyes of some toads.

Burrow
A tunnel excavated and inhabited by an animal.

Carnivorous
Feeding primarily on meat.

Catkin
A caterpillar-like drooping cluster of small flowers.

Cold-blooded
Refers to animals that are unable to regulate their own body temperature. 'Ectotherm' is the preferred term for this characteristic since many 'cold-blooded' species like reptiles are at times able to maintain a warmer body temperature than that of 'warm-blooded' species like mammals.

Conifer
A cone-bearing tree, usually evergreen.

Coral
The limestone skeletal deposits of coral polyps.

Coverts
Small feathers that cover the underside (undertail) or top (uppertail) of the base of a bird's tail.

Deciduous
Shedding leaves annually.

Diurnal
Active primarily during the day.

Dorsal
Pertaining to the back or upper surface.

Ecology
The study of the relationships between organisms, and between organisms and their environment.

Endangered
Species threatened with extinction.

Epiphyte
A plant that obtains nourishment from nutrients in the air and rain. They often live on host plants like trees without harming them.

Endemic
Living only in a particular area.

Flower
Reproductive structure of a plant.

Flower stalk
The stem bearing the flowers.

Fruit
The matured, seed-bearing ovary.

Gamete
An egg or sperm cell.

Habitat
The physical area in which organisms live.

Herbivorous
Feeding primarily on vegetation.

Insectivorous
Feeding primarily on insects.

Introduced
Species brought by humans to an area outside its normal range.

Invertebrate
Animals lacking backbones, e.g., worms, slugs, crustaceans, insects, shellfish.

Larva
Immature forms of an animal that differ from the adult.

Lateral
Located away from the mid-line, at or near the sides.

Lobe
A projecting part of a leaf or flower, usually rounded.

Mesa
High, flat-topped mountain or hill with steeply sloping sides.

Molting
Loss of feathers, hair or skin while renewing plumage, coat or scales.

Morphs
A color variation of a species that is regular and not related to sex, age or season.

Nest
A structure built for shelter or insulation.

Nocturnal
Active primarily at night.

Omnivorous
Feeding on both animal and vegetable food.

Ovary
The female sex organ that is the site of egg production and maturation.

Perennial
A plant that lives for several years.

Petal
The colored outer parts of a flower head.

Phase
Coloration other than typical.

Pistil
The central organ of the flower that develops into a fruit.

Pollen
The tiny grains produced in the anthers that contain the male reproductive cells.

Posterior
Pertaining to the rear.

Sepal
The outer, usually green, leaf-like structures that protect the flower bud and are located at the base of an open flower.

Species
A group of interbreeding organisms that are reproductively isolated from other groups.

Speculum
A brightly colored, iridescent patch on the wings of some birds, especially ducks.

Spur
A pointed projection.

Subspecies
A relatively uniform, distinct portion of a species population.

Terrestrial
Land dwelling.

Threatened
Species not yet endangered but in imminent danger of being so.

Ungulate
An animal that has hooves.

Ventral
Pertaining to the under or lower surface.

Vertebrate
An animal possessing a backbone.

Warm-blooded
An animal that regulates its blood temperature internally. 'Endotherm' is the preferred term for this characteristic.

Whorl
A circle of leaves or flowers about a stem.

Woolly
Bearing long or matted hairs.

MAMMALS

Armstrong, D. M. and Fitzgerald, J. P. *Mammals of Colorado. 2ⁿᵈ. Ed.* Louisville: University Press of Colorado, 2010.

Whitaker, John O., Jr. *National Audubon Society Field Guide to North American Mammals.* Rev. ed. New York: Alfred A. Knopf, 1996.

Reid, F. A. *Mammals of North America.* Boston: Houghton Mifflin, 2006.

Kaufmann, K. and Bowers, R. *Mammals of North America.* New York: Houghton Mifflin, 2007.

Rennicke, J. *Colorado Wildlife.* Helena: Falcon Press. 1996.

Murie, Olaus J. A Field Guide to *Animal Tracks.* New York: Houghton Mifflin, 1998.

Elbroch, Mark. *Mammal Tracks & Sign.* Mechanicsburg, PA: Stackpole Books. 2019.

Stokes, D. and Stokes, Lillian. *Stokes Guide to Animal Tracking and Behavior.* New York: Little Brown. 2018.

Farrand, John. Jr. *Familiar Animal Tracks.* New York: Alfred A Knopf. 1995.

BIRDS

Holt, H. *A Birder's Guide to Colorado.* Colorado Springs: American Birding Association. 2006.

National Geographic Field Guide to the Birds of North America. 7th ed. Washington, D.C.: National Geographic Society, 2017.

Sibley, David Allen. *The Sibley Guide to Birds.* New York: Alfred A. Knopf, 2014.

Udvardy, Miklos D.F. *The Audubon Society Field Guide to North American Birds: Western Region.* New York: Alfred A. Knopf, 1994.

Peterson, Roger Tory. *A Field Guide to Western Birds.* 3rd ed. Boston: Houghton Mifflin, 2010.

Alsop, Fred J., III. *Smithsonian Handbooks Birds of North America: Western Region.* New York: Dorling Kindersley, 2001.

Kavanagh, J. and Leung, R. *Birds of Colorado.* Tampa: Waterford Press. 2017.

Reptiles & Amphibians

Behler, J. L. and King, W. F. *The Audubon Society Field Guide to North American Reptiles and Amphibians.* New York: Alfred A. Knopf, 1998.

Stebbins, R. C. and Peterson, R. T. *A Peterson Field Guide to Western Reptiles and Amphibians.* Boston: Houghton Mifflin, 2003.

Young, M. T. *The Guide to Colorado Reptiles and Amphibians.* Golden: Fulcrum Publishing. 2011.

REPTILES & AMPHIBIANS

Hammerson, G.A. *Amphibians and Reptiles in Colorado.* Loisville, CO: University Press of Colorado, 1999.

Young, M.T. *The Guide to Colorado Reptiles and Amphibians.* Golden: Fulcrum Publishing, 2011.

Behler, J. L. and King, W. F. *The Audubon Society Field Guide to North American Reptiles and Amphibians.* New York: Alfred A. Knopf, 1998.

Conant, R. and Powell, R. *Peterson Field Guide to Reptiles and Amphibians of Eastern and Central North America.* Boston: Houghton Mifflin, 2016.

FISHES

Johnson, D. *Fish of Colorado.* Cambridge: Adventure Publications, 2007.

Behnke, R. J. and Tomelleri, J. R. *Trout and Salmon of North America.* New York: The Free Press, 2002.

Gilbert, Carter R. and Williams, James D. *National Audubon Society Field Guide to Fishes: North America.* Rev. ed. New York: Alfred A. Knopf, 2002.

Page, Lawrence and Burr, Brooks M. *A Field Guide to Freshwater Fishes: North America North of Mexico.* Boston: Houghton Mifflin, 1991.

BUTTERFLIES & MOTHS

Carter, David. *Eyewitness Handbooks: Butterflies and Moths.* New York: Dorling Kindersley, 1992.

Farrand, John, Jr., ed. *National Audubon Society Pocket Guide: Insects and Spiders.* New York: Alfred A. Knopf, 1995.

Milne, Lorus and Milne, Margery. *National Audubon Society Field Guide to North American Insects and Spiders.* New York: Alfred A. Knopf, 2000.

Kavanagh, J. and Leung, R. *Colorado Butterflies and Moths.* Tampa: Waterford Press. 2018.

TREES, SHRUBS & CACTI

Tekiela, S. *Trees of Colorado.* Cambridge: Adventure Publications, 2007.

Elias, Thomas S. *The Complete Trees of North America.* New York: Van Nostrand Reinhold, 1987.

Little, Elbert L. *National Audubon Society Field Guide to North American Trees: Western Region.* New York: Alfred A. Knopf, 1980.

WILDFLOWERS

Mammoser, D. *Wildflowers of Colorado.* Cambridge: Adventure Publications, 2007.

Spellenberg, R. *The Audubon Society Field Guide to North American Wildflowers – Western Region.* New York: Alfred A. Knopf, 2001.

Jones, C. F. *Colorado Wildflowers.* Helena: Falcon Press, 1994.

Venning, D. *Wildflowers of North America.* New York: Golden Press, 1984.

NATURAL HISTORY

Fleisher C. and Emerick J. *Grassland to Glacier.* Boulder: Johnson Printing. 1992.

Young, Mary Taylor. *Colorado Wildlife Viewing Guide.* St. Croix: Watchable Wildlife Inc. 2007.

Kruger, F.A. and Meaney, C.A. *Explore Colorado: A Naturalists Notebook.* Denver: Denver Museum of Natural History. 1995.

Alden, P. and Grassy, J. *National Audubon Society Field Guide to the Rocky Mountain States.* New York: Random House. 1999.

MAIN WEB RESOURCES:

Colorado Parks and Wildlife – cpw.state.co.us

Colorado Division of Wildlife – wildlife.state.co.us

USDA Plants Database – plants.usda.gov/about_plants.html

Colorado State University Herbarium – herbarium.biology.colostate.edu/

Denver Museum of Nature and Science – www.dmns.org

Coloradobirdingtrail.com

OSMP Wildlife Overview – www.bouldercolorado.gov